YOU ARE THE WORLD

YOU ARE THE WORLD

Authentic Report of Talks and
Discussions in American Universities

J. KRISHNAMURTI

*"In oneself lies the whole world, and if
you know how to look and learn, then the
door is there and the key is in your hand.
Nobody on earth can give you either that
key or the door to open, except yourself."*

(page 135)

Harper & Row, Publishers
New York, Evanston, San Francisco, London

First PERENNIAL LIBRARY edition published in 1973.

STANDARD BOOK NUMBER: 06–08030–7

3–75

CONTENTS

THREE TALKS AT BRANDEIS UNIVERSITY

I

As one travels one is very much aware that human problems everywhere, though apparently dissimilar, are really more or less similar: the problems of violence and the problem of freedom; the problem of how to bring about a real and better relationship between man and man, so that he may live at peace, with some decency and not be constantly in conflict, not only within himself but also with his neighbor. Also there is the problem, as in the whole of Asia, of poverty, starvation and the utter despair of the poor. And there is the problem, as in this country and in Western Europe, of prosperity; where there is prosperity without austerity there is violence, there is every form of unethical luxury—the society which is utterly corrupt and immoral.

There is the problem of organized religion—which man, throughout the world is rejecting, more or less—and the question of what a religious mind is and what meditation is —which are not monopolies of the East. There is the question of love and death—so many interrelated problems. The speaker does not represent any system of conceptual thinking or ideology, Indian or otherwise. If we can talk over together these many problems, not as with an expert or a specialist—because the speaker is neither—then possibly we can establish right communication; but bear in mind that the word is not the thing, and that the description, however detailed, however intricate, however well-reasoned out and beautiful, is not the thing described.

There are the whole separate worlds, the ideological divisions of the Hindu, the Muslim, the Christian and the Communist, which have brought about such incalculable harm, such hatred and antagonism. All ideologies are idiotic, whether religious or political, for it is conceptual thinking, the conceptual word, which has so unfortunately divided man.

These ideologies have brought about wars; although there may be religious tolerance, it is up to a certain point only; after that, destruction, intolerance, brutality, violence —the religious wars. Similarly there are the national and tribal divisions caused by ideologies, the black nationalism and the various tribal expressions.

Is it at all possible to live in this world nonviolently, in freedom, virtuously? Freedom is absolutely necessary; but not freedom for the individual to do what he likes to do, because the individual is conditioned—whether he is living in this country or in India or anywhere else—he is conditioned by his society, by his culture, by the whole structure of his thought. Is it at all possible to be free from this conditioning, not ideologically, not as an idea, but actually psychologically, inwardly, free?—otherwise I do not see how there can be any democracy or any righteous behavior. Again, the expression "righteous behavior" is rather looked down upon, but I hope we can use these words to convey what is meant without any derogatory sense.

Freedom is not an idea; a philosophy written about freedom is not freedom. Either one is free or one is not. One is in a prison, however decorative that prison is; a prisoner is free only when he is no longer in prison. Freedom is not a state of the mind that is caught in thought. Thought can never be free. Thought is the response of memory, knowledge and experience; it is always the product of the past and it cannot possibly bring about freedom because freedom is something that is in the living active present, in

2

daily life. Freedom is *not freedom from* something—freedom *from* something is merely a reaction.

Why has man given such extraordinary importance to thought?—thought which formulates a concept according to which he tries to live. The formulation of ideologies and the attempted conformity to those ideologies is observable throughout the world. The Hitler movement did it, the Communist people are doing it very thoroughly; the religious groups, the Catholics, the Protestants, the Hindus, and so on have asserted their ideologies through propaganda, for two thousand years, and have made man conform through threats, through promises. One observes this phenomenon throughout the world; man has always given thought such extraordinary significance and importance. The more specialized, the more intellectual, the more thought becomes of serious import. So we ask: Can thought ever solve our human problems?

There is the problem of violence, not only the student revolt in Paris, Rome, London and Columbia, here and in the rest of the world, but this spreading of hatred and violence, black against white, Hindu against Muslim. There is the incredible brutality and extraordinary violence that human hearts carry—though outwardly educated, conditioned, to repeat prayers of peace. Human beings are extraordinarily violent. This violence is the result of political and racial divisions and of religious distinctions.

This violence that is so embedded in each human being, can one actually transform it, change it completely, so that one lives at peace? This violence man has obviously inherited from the animal and from the society in which he lives. Man is committed to war, man accepts war as the way of life; there may be a few pacifists here and there, carrying antiwar slogans, but there are those who love war and have favorite wars! There are those who may not approve of the Vietnamese War but they will fight for something else, they will have another kind of war. Man has actually accepted war, that is, conflict, not only within himself but outwardly, as a way of life.

3

What the human being is, totally, both at the conscious as well as at the deeper levels of his consciousness, produces a society with a corresponding structure—which is obvious. And one asks again: Is it at all possible for man, having accustomed himself through education, through acceptance of the social norm and culture, to bring about a psychological revolution within himself?—not a mere outward revolution.

Is it at all possible to bring about a psychological revolution immediately?—not in time, not gradually, because there is no time when the house is burning; you do not talk about gradually putting out the fire; you have no time, time is a delusion. So what will make man change? What will make either you or me as a human being, change? Motive, either of reward or punishment? That has been tried. Psychological rewards, the promise of heaven, the punishment of hell, we have had in abundance and apparently man has not changed, he is still envious, greedy, violent, superstitious, fearful and so on. Mere motive, whether it is given outwardly or inwardly, does not bring about a radical change. Finding, through analysis, the cause why man is so violent, so full of fear, so greatly acquisitive, competitive, so violently ambitious—which is fairly easy—will that bring about a change? Obviously not, neither that nor the uncovering of the motive. Then what will? What will bring about, not gradually, but immediately, the psychological revolution? That, it seems to me, is the only issue.

Analysis—analysis by the specialist, or introspective analysis—does not answer the issue. Analysis takes time, it requires a great deal of insight, for if you analyze wrongly the following analysis will be wrong. If you analyze and come to a conclusion and proceed from that conclusion then you are already stymied, you are already blocked. And in analysis there is the problem of the "analyzer" and the "analyzed."

How is this radical, fundamental change to be brought about psychologically, inwardly if not through motive, or

4

through analysis and the discovery of the cause? One can easily find out why one is angry, but that does not stop one from being angry. One can find out what the contributory causes of war are, be they economic, national, religious, or the pride of the politicians, the ideologies, the commitments and so on, yet we go on killing each other, in the name of God, in the name of an ideology, in the name of country, in the name of whatever it is. There have been 15,000 wars in 5,000 years!—still we have no love, no compassion!

In penetrating this question one comes upon the inevitable problem of the "analyzer" and that which is "analyzed," the "thinker" and the "thought," the "observer" and the "observed," and the problem of whether this division between the "observer" and the "observed" is real, real in the sense of being an actual problem and not something theoretical. Is the "observer"—the center from which you look, from which you see, from which you listen—a conceptual entity who has separated himself from the observed? When one says one is angry, is the anger different from the entity who knows he is angry?—is violence separate from the "observer?" Is not violence part of the observer? Please, this is a very important thing to understand. The central thing to understand, when we are concerned with this question of immediate psychological change—not change in some future state or at some future time. Is the "observer," the "me," the "ego," the "thinker," the "experiencer," different from the thing, the experience, the thought, which he observes? When you look at that tree, when you see the bird on the wing, the evening light on the water, is the "experiencer" different from that which he observes? Do we, when we look at a tree, ever "look" at it? Please do go with me a little. Do we ever look directly at it? —or do we look at it through the imagery of knowledge, of the past experience that we have had? You say, "Yes, I know what a lovely color it is, how beautiful the shape is." You remember it and then enjoy the pleasure derived through that memory, through the memory of the feeling of closeness to it and so on. Have you ever observed the "observer" as different from the observed? Unless one goes into this profoundly what follows may be missed. As long as there is a division between the "observer" and the "observed" there is conflict. The division, spatial and verbal, that comes into the mind with the imagery, the knowledge, the memory of last year's autumnal colors, creates the "observer" and the division from the observed is conflict. Thought brings about this division. You look at your neighbor, at your wife, at your husband or your boyfriend or girlfriend, whoever it be, but can you look without the imagery of thought, without the previous memory? For when you look with an image there is no relationship; there is merely the indirect relationship between the two groups of images, of the woman or of the man, about each other; there is conceptual relationship, not actual relationship.

We live in a world of concepts, in a world of thought. We try to solve all our problems, from the most mechanical to psychological problems of the greatest depth, by means of thought.

If there is a division between the "observer" and the "observed" that division is the source of all human conflict. When you say you love somebody, is that love? For in that love is there not both the "observer" and the thing you love, the observed? That "love" is the product of thought, divided off as a concept and there is not love.

Is thought the only instrument that we have to deal with all our human problems?—for it does not answer, it does not resolve our problems. It may be, we are just questioning it, we are not dogmatically asserting it. It may be that thought has no place whatsoever, except for mechanical, technological, scientific matters.

When the "observer" is the "observed" then conflict ceases. This happens quite normally, quite easily: in circumstances when there is great danger there is no "observer" separate from the "observed"; there is immediate action, there is instant response in action. When there is a great crisis in one's life—and one always avoids great crises —one has no time to think about it. In such circumstance the brain, with all its memories of the old, does not immediately respond, yet there is immediate action. There is an immediate change, psychologically, inwardly, when the division of the "observer" from the "observed" comes to an end. To put it differently: one lives in the past, all knowledge is of the past. One lives there, one's life is there, in what has been—concerned with "what I was" and from that, "what I shall be." One's life is based essentially on yesterday and "yesterday" makes us invulnerable, deprives us of the capacity of innocency, vulnerability. So "yesterday" is the "observer"; in the "observer" are all the layers of the unconscious as well as the conscious.

The whole of humankind is in each one of us, in both the conscious and the unconscious, the deeper layers. One is the result of thousands of years; embedded in each one of us—as one can find if one knows how to delve into it, go deeply inside—is the whole history, the whole knowledge, of the past. That is why self-knowledge is immensely important. "Oneself" is now secondhand; one repeats what others have told us, whether it be Freud or whoever the specialist. If one wants to know oneself one cannot look through the eyes of the specialist; one has to look directly at oneself.

How can one know oneself without being an "observer"? What do we mean by "knowing"?—I am not quibbling about words—what do we mean by "knowing," to "know"? When do I "know" something? I say I "know" Sanskrit, I "know" Latin—or I say I "know" my wife or husband. Knowing a language is different from "knowing" my wife or husband. I learn to know a language but can I ever say I know my wife?—or husband? When I say I "know" my wife it is that I have an image about her: but that image is always in the past; that image prevents me from looking at her—she may already be changing. So can I ever say I "know"? When one asks, "Can I know myself without the observer?"—see what takes place.

7

It is rather complex: I learn about myself; in learning about myself I accumulate knowledge about myself and use that knowledge, which is of the past, to learn something more about myself. *With the accumulated knowledge I have about myself I look at myself and I try to learn something new about myself.* Can I do that? It is impossible.

To learn about myself and to know about myself: the two things are entirely different. Learning is a constant, nonaccumulative process, and "myself" is something changing all the time, new thoughts, new feelings, new variations, new intimations, new hints. To learn is not something related to the past or the future; I cannot say I have learned and I am going to learn. So the mind must be in a constant state of learning, therefore always in the active present, always fresh; not stale with the accumulated knowledge of yesterday. Then you will see, if you go into it, that there is only learning and not the acquiring of knowledge; then the mind becomes extraordinarily alert, aware and sharp to look. I can never say I "know" about myself: and any person who says, "I know," obviously does not know. Learning is a constant, active process; it is not a matter of having learned. I learn more in order to add to what I have already learned. To learn about myself there must be freedom to look and this freedom to look is denied when I look through the knowledge of yesterday.

Questioner: Why does the separation between the "observer" and the "observed" lead to conflict?

KRISHNAMURTI: Who is the maker of effort? Conflict exists as long as there is effort, as long as there is contradiction. So, is there not a contradiction between the "observer" and the "observed"—in that division? This is not a matter of argument or opinion—you can look at it. When I say "This is mine"—whether property, whether sexual rights, or whether it is my work—there is a resistance which separates and therefore there is conflict. When I say "I am a Hindu," "I am Brahmin," this and that, I have created a world around myself with which I have identified myself which breeds division. Surely, when one says one is a Catholic, one has already separated oneself from the non-Catholics. All division, outwardly as well as inwardly, breeds antagonism. So the problem arises, can I own anything without creating antagonism, without creating this definite contradiction, which breeds conflict? Or is there a different dimension altogether where the sense of nonownership exists, and therefore there is freedom?

Questioner: Is it possible to act at all without having mental concepts? Could you have even walked into this room and sat down in that chair without having a concept of what a chair is? You seem to be implying that there need be no concepts at all.

KRISHNAMURTI: Perhaps I may not have explained it in sufficient detail. One must have concepts. If I ask you where you live, unless you are in a state of amnesia, you will tell me. The "telling me" is born of a concept, of a remembrance—and one must have such remembrances, concepts. But it is the concepts that have bred ideologies which are the source of mischief: You, an American, I, a Hindu, Indian. You are committed to one ideology and I am committed to another ideology. These ideologies are conceptual and we are willing to kill each other for them though we may cooperate scientifically, in the laboratory. But in human relationship, has conceptual thinking any place? This is a more complex problem. All reaction is conceptual, all reaction: I have an idea and according to that idea I act; that is, first an idea, a formula, a norm, and then according to that an action. So there is a division between the concept, or idea, and the action. The conceptual side of this division is the "observer." The action is something outside us and hence the division, conflict. That raises the question as to whether a mind that has been conditioned, educated, brought up socially, can free itself from conceptual thinking and yet act nonmechanically. Can a mind be in a state of silence and act, can it operate without concepts? I say it is possible; but it has no value because I say so. I say it is possible and that that is meditation: To resolve this question as to whether the mind—the whole mind—can be utterly silent, free from conceptual thinking, free from thinking altogether, so that only when thought is necessary does it think. I am talking English, there is an automatic process going on. Can you listen to me completely silently, without any interference of thought?—seeing that the moment you *try* to do this you are already in thought. Is it possible to look—at a tree, at the microphone —without the word, the word being the thought, the concept? To look at a tree without a concept is fairly easy. But to look at a friend, to look at somebody who has hurt you, who has flattered you, to look without a word, without a concept is more difficult; it means that the brain is quiet, it has its responses, its reactions, it is quick, but it is so quiet that it can look completely, totally, out of silence. It is only in that state that you understand and act with an action that is nonfragmentary.

Questioner: Yes, I think I know what you are saying.

KRISHNAMURTI: Good, but you have to do it. One has to know oneself; then arises the problem of the "observer" and the "observed," "analyzer" and "analyzed" and so on. There is a look without all this, which is instant understanding.

Questioner: You are trying to communicate with words something which you say it is impossible to do with words.

KRISHNAMURTI: There is verbal communication because you and I, both of us, understand English. To communicate with each other properly you and I must both be urgent and have the capacity, the quality of intensity, at the same time—otherwise we do not communicate. If you are looking out of the window and I am talking, or if you are serious and I am not serious, then communication ceases. Now, to communicate something which you or I have not gone into is extremely difficult. But there is a communication which is not verbal, which comes about when you and I are both serious, both intense and immediate, at the same time, at the same level; then there is "communion" which

10

is nonverbal. Then we can dispense with words. Then you and I can sit in silence; but it must be not my silence or your silence, but that of both of us; then perhaps there can be communion. But that is asking too much.

2

We have so many complex problems; unfortunately we rely on others, experts and specialists, to solve them. Religions throughout the world have offered various forms of escape from them. It was thought that science would help to resolve this complexity of human problems; that education would resolve and put an end to them. But one observes that the problems are increasing throughout the world, they are multiplying and becoming more and more urgent, complex, and seemingly endless. Eventually one realizes that one cannot depend on anyone, either on the priests, the scientists or the specialists. One has to "go it alone" for they have all failed; the wars, the divisions of religion, the antagonism of man to man, the brutalities, all continue; constant and progressive fear and sorrow exist.

One sees that one has to make the journey of understanding by oneself; one sees that there is no "authority." Every form of "authority" (except, at a different level, the authority of the technocrats and the specialists) has failed. Man set up these "authorities" as a guide, as a means of bringing freedom, peace, and because they have failed they have lost their meaning and hence there is a general revolt against the "authorities," spiritual, moral and ethical. Everything is breaking down. One can see in this country, which is quite young, perhaps 300 years old, that there is already a decay taking place before maturity has been reached; there is disorder, conflict, confusion; there is inevitable fear and sorrow. These outward events inevitably force one to find for oneself the answer; one has to wipe the slate clean and begin again, knowing that no outside authority is going to help, no belief, no religious sanction, no moral standard—nothing. The inheritance from the past, with its Scriptures, its Savior, is no longer important. One is forced to stand alone, examining, exploring, questioning, doubting everything, so that one's own mind becomes clarified; so that it is no longer conditioned, perverted, tortured.

Can we in fact stand alone and explore for ourselves to find the right answer? Can we, in exploring our own minds, our own hearts which are so heavily conditioned, be free, completely—both unconsciously as well as consciously?

Can the mind be free of fear? This is one of the major issues of life. Can the human mind ever be free from the contagion of fear? Let us go into it, not abstractly, not theoretically, but by actually being aware of one's own fears, physical as well as psychological, conscious as well as the secret hidden fears. Is that possible? One may be aware of the physical fears—that is fairly simple. But can one be aware of the unconscious, deeper layers of fears?

Fear in any form darkens the mind, perverts the mind, brings about confusion and neurotic states. In fear there is no clarity. And let us bear in mind that one can theorize about the causes of fear, analyze them very carefully, go into them intellectually, but at the end one is still afraid. But if one could go into this question of fear, being actually aware of it, then perhaps we could be free of it completely.

There are the conscious fears: "I am afraid of public opinion"; "I might lose my job"; "my wife may run away"; "I am afraid of being lonely"; "I am afraid of not being loved"; "I am afraid of dying." There is fear of the apparently meaningless boredom of this life, the everlasting trap in which one is caught; the tedium of being educated, earning a livelihood in an office or in a factory, bearing children, the enjoyment of a few sexual interludes and the inevitable sorrow and death. All this engenders fear, conscious fear. Can one face all this fear, go through it, so that one is no longer afraid. Can one brush all that aside and be free? If one cannot, then obviously one lives in a state of perpetual anxiety, guilt, uncertainty, with increasing and multiplying problems.

So, what is fear? Do we really know fear at all, or do we know it only when it is over? It is important to find this out. Are we ever directly in contact with fear, or is our mind so accustomed, so trained, that it is always escaping and so never coming directly into contact with what it calls fear? It would be worthwhile if you could take your own fear and as we go into it together perhaps we may learn directly about fear.

What is fear? How does it come about? What is the structure and nature of fear? One is, for example, afraid, as we said, of public opinion; there are several things involved in that: one might lose one's job and so on. How does this fear arise? Is it the result of time? Does fear come to an end when I know the cause of fear? Does fear disappear through analysis, in exploring and finding out its cause? I am afraid of something, of death, of what might happen the day after tomorrow, or I am afraid of the past; what sustains and gives continuity to this fear? One may have done something wrong, or one may have said something which should not have been said, *all in the past*; or one is afraid of what might happen, ill health, disease, losing one's job, *all in the future*. So there is fear of the *past* and there is fear of the *future*. Fear of the past is the fear of something which has actually taken place and fear of the future is the fear of something which might happen, a possibility.

What sustains and gives continuity to the fear of the past and also to the fear for the future? Surely it is thought —thought of what one has done in the past, or of how a particular disease has given pain and one is afraid of the future repetition of that pain. Fear is sustained by memory, by thinking about it. Thought, in thinking about past pain or pleasure, gives a continuity to it, sustains and nourishes it. Pleasure or pain in relation to the future is the activity of thought.

I am afraid of something I have done, its possible consequences in the future. This fear is sustained by thought. That is fairly obvious. So thought is time—psychologically. Thought brings about psychological time as distinct from chronological time. (We are not talking about chronological time.)

Thought, which puts together time as yesterday, today and tomorrow, breeds fear. Thought creates the interval between now and what might happen in the future. Thought perpetuates fear through psychological time; thought is the origin of fear; thought is the source of sorrow. Do we accept this? Do we actually see the nature of thought, how it operates, how it functions and produces the whole structure of the past, present and the future? Do we see that thought, through analysis, discovering the causes of fear, which takes time, cannot dissolve fear? In the interval between the cause of fear and the ending of fear there is the action of fear. It is like a man who is violent and has invented the ideology of nonviolence; he says "I will become nonviolent," but in the meantime he is sowing the seeds of violence. So, if we use time—time which is thought—as a means of being free of fear, we will not resolve fear. Fear is not to be resolved by thought because thought has bred fear.

So what is one to do? If thought is not the way out of this trap of fear—do understand this very clearly, not intellectually, not verbally, not as an argument with which you agree or disagree, but as one who is concerned, involved in this question of fear, deeply as we must be if we are at all serious—then, what is one to do? Thought is responsible for fear; thought breeds both fear and pleasure. If one sees very clearly that thought breeds this enormous sense of fear and that thought cannot possibly solve this fear, then what is the next step? I hope you are asking this question of yourself and not waiting for me to answer it. If you are not waiting for me to answer it, then you are up against it, it is a challenge and you must answer it. If you answer that challenge with the old responses, then where

14

are you?—you are still afraid. The challenge is new, immediate: *thought has bred fear and thought cannot possibly end fear; what will you do?*

First of all, when one says "I have understood the whole nature and structure of thought," what does one mean by that? What does one mean by "I understand," "I have understood it," "I have seen the nature of thought"? What is the state of the mind, which says, "I have understood"?

Please follow carefully, do not assert anything. We are asking: *does thought understand?* You tell me something, you describe for example the complexity of modern life very carefully, minutely, and I say, "I have understood," not merely the description but the content, the depth, so that I see how human beings caught in it are in a nervous, neurotic, terrible state and so on. I have understood with feeling, with my nerves, with my ears, everything, so that I am no longer caught in it. It is as when I have understood that a cobra is dangerous—then, finished, I won't go near it. My action if I do meet it will be entirely different now that I have understood it.

So, is one in a state of understanding the nature of thought and the product of thought, which is fear and pleasure? Has one come to grips with it? Has one seen, actually, not theoretically or verbally or intellectually, how it operates? Or, am I still with the description, am I still with the argument, with the logical sequence, and not with the fact? If I am merely content with the description, with the verbal explanation, then I am just playing around with it. When the description has led me to the thing described there is direct perception of it; then there is quite a different action. (It is like a hungry man who wants food, not a description of food or the conclusion as to what would happen if he ate; he wants food.)

When one sees how thought breeds fear, then what takes place? When one is hungry and someone describes how lovely food is, what does one do, what is one's response? One will say, "Don't describe food to me, give it me." The action is there, direct, not theoretical. So when one

15

says "I understand," it means that there is a constant movement of learning about thought and fear and pleasure; from this constant movement one acts; one acts in the very movement of learning. When there is such learning about fear there is the ending of fear.

There are fears which the mind has never uncovered, hidden, secret. How can the conscious mind uncover them? The conscious mind receives the hints of those fears through dreams; when one has these dreams, have they to be interpreted? As one cannot understand them for oneself easily one may have an outside interpreter, but he will interpret them according to his particular method or specialization. And there are those dreams that, as one is dreaming, one is interpreting.

Why should one dream at all? The specialists say one must dream or one will go crazy; but I am not at all sure that one must dream. Why cannot one, during the day, be open to the hints and intimations of the unconscious, so that one does not dream at all? While this constant struggle of dreaming goes on in sleep, one's mind is never quiet, never refreshed, never renewed. Cannot the mind during the day be so open, so alert, awake and aware, that the hints and intimations of the hidden fears can come out and be observed and absorbed?

Through awareness, through attention during the day, in speech, in act, in everything that takes place, then both the hidden and the open fears are exposed; then when you sleep there is a sleep that is completely quiet, without a single dream and the mind wakes up the next morning fresh, young, innocent, alive. This is not a theory—do it and you will find out.

Questioner: How is it possible to bring the hidden fears out into consciousness?

KRISHNAMURTI: One can observe within oneself if one is alert, quick, watchful, that the unconscious is, among other things, the repository of the past, the racial inheritance. I was born in India, raised in a certain class as a Brahmin, with all its prejudices, superstitions, its strict moral life and so on, together with all the racial and the family content, the tradition of ten thousand years and more, collective and individual, it is all there in the unconscious. That is what we generally mean by the unconscious; the specialist may give it another meaning but as laymen we can observe it for ourselves. Now, how is all that to be exposed? How will you do it? There is the unconscious in you; if you are a Jew there is all the tradition, hidden, of Judaism; if you are a Catholic, there is all that there, hidden, if you are a Communist it is there in a different way, and so on. Now how will you, without dreaming—it is not a puzzle—how will you bring all that into the open?

If during the day you are alert, aware of all the movement of thought, aware of what you are saying, your gestures, how you sit, how you walk, how you talk, aware of your responses, then all the hidden things come out very easily; and it will not take time, it will not take many days, for you are no longer resisting, you are no longer actively digging, you are just observing, listening. In that state of awareness everything is exposed. But if you say, "I will keep some things and I will discard others," you are half asleep. If you say, "I will keep all the 'goodness' of Hinduism or Judaism or Catholicism and let the rest go," obviously you are still conditioned, holding on. So one has to let all this come out, without resistance.

Questioner: That awareness is without choice?

KRISHNAMURTI: If that awareness is "choosing," then you are blocking it. But if that awareness is without choice, everything is exposed, the most hidden and secret demands, fears and compulsions.

Questioner: Should one attempt to be aware for one hour a day?

KRISHNAMURTI: If I am aware, if I am attentive, for one minute, that is enough. Most of us are inattentive. To become aware of that inattention is attention; but the cultivation of attention is not attention. I am aware for a single minute of everything that is going on in me, without any choice, observing very clearly; then I spend an hour not giving attention; I take it up again at the end of the hour.

3

I was told the other day that meditation has no place in America at the present time; that the Americans need action, not meditation. I wonder why this division is made between a contemplative, meditative life and a life of action. We are caught in this dualistic, fragmented way of looking at life. In India there is the concept of various ways of life; the man of action, the man of knowledge, the man of wisdom and so on. Such division in the very act of living must inevitably lead to conformity, limitation and contradiction.

If we are to go into this question of meditation—which is an extraordinarily complex and, for the speaker, most important thing—we have to understand what we mean by that word. The dictionary meaning of that word is "to ponder over," "think over," "consider," "inquire thoughtfully," and so on. India and Asia seem to have monopolized that word as though meditation in all its depth, meaning and the very end of it, is under their control; the monopoly apparently is with them—which of course is absurd. When we speak of "meditation" we must be clear as to whether it is with the intent to escape from life—the daily grind, the boredom, anxiety and fear—or as a way of life. Either, through meditation, we seek to escape altogether from this mad and ugly world or it is the very understanding, living and acting in life itself. If we want to escape then there are various schools: the Zen Monasteries in Japan and the many other systems. We can see why they are so tempting, for life, as it is, is very ugly, brutal, competitive, ruthless; it has no meaning whatsoever, as it is.

When the Hindus offer their systems of Yoga, their mantras, the repetition of words and so on, we may obviously be tempted to accept rather easily and without much thought, for they promise a reward, a sense of satisfaction in escape. So let us be very clear; we are not concerned with any escape, either through a contemplative, visionary life, through drugs or the repetition of words.

In India, the repetition of certain Sanskrit words is called mantra; they have a special tonality and are said to make the mind more vibrant, alive. But the repetition of these mantras must make the mind dull; maybe that is what most human beings want, they cannot face life as it is, it is too appalling and they want to be made insensitive. The repetition of words and the taking of drugs, drink and so on, does help to dull the mind. The dulling of the mind is called "quietness," "silence," which it obviously is not. A dull mind can think about God and virtue and beauty yet remain dull, stupid and heavy. We are not concerned in any way with these various forms of escape.

Meditation is not a fragmentation of life; it is not a withdrawal into a monastery or into a room, sitting quietly for ten minutes or an hour, trying to concentrate, to learn to meditate, and yet for the rest being a hideous, ugly human being. One brushes all that aside as being unintelligent, as belonging to a state of mind that is incapable of really perceiving what truth is; for to understand what truth is one must have a very sharp, clear, precise mind; not a cunning mind, not tortured, but a mind that is capable of looking without any distortion, a mind innocent and vulnerable; only such a mind that can see what truth is. Nor can a mind that is filled with knowledge perceive what truth is; only a mind that is completely capable of learning can do that; learning is not the accumulation of knowledge; learning is a movement from moment to moment. The mind and the body also must be highly sensitive. You cannot have a dull, heavy body, loaded with wine and meat, and then try to mediate—that has no meaning. So the mind—if one goes into this question very seriously and deeply—must be highly alert, highly sensitive and intelligent, not the intelligence born of knowledge.

Living in this world with all its travail, so caught up in misery, sorrow and violence, is it possible to bring the mind to a state that is highly sensitive and intelligent? That is the first and an essential point in meditation. Second: a mind that is capable of logical, sequential perception, in no way distorted or neurotic. Third: a mind that is highly disciplined. The word "discipline" means "to learn," not to be drilled. "Discipline" is an act of learning—the very root of the word means that. A disciplined mind sees everything very clearly, objectively, not emotionally, not sentimentally. Those are the basic necessities to discover that which is beyond the measure of thought, something not put together by thought, capable of the highest form of love, a dimension that is not the projection of one's own little mind.

We have created society and that society has conditioned us. Our minds are tortured and heavily conditioned by a morality which is not moral; the morality of society is immorality, because society admits and encourages violence, greed, competition, ambition and so on, which are essentially immoral. There is no love, consideration, affection, tenderness, and the "moral respectability" of society is utterly disorderly. A mind that has been trained for thousands of years to accept, to obey and conform, cannot possibly be highly sensitive and therefore highly virtuous. We are caught in this trap. So then, what is virtue?—because that is necessary.

Without the right foundation a mathematician does not go very far. In the same way, if one would understand and go beyond to something which is of a totally different dimension, one must lay the right foundation; and the right foundation is virtue, which is order—not the order of society which is disorder. Without order, how can the mind be sensitive, alive, free?

Virtue is obviously not the repetitive behavior of conforming to a pattern which has become respectable, which the establishment, whether in this country or the rest of the world, accepts as morality. One must be very clear on this point as to what virtue is. One comes upon virtue; it cannot be cultivated any more than one can cultivate love, or humility. One comes upon it—the nature of virtue, its beauty, its orderliness—when one knows what it is not; through negation one finds out what is positive. One does not come upon virtue by defining the positive and then imitating it—that is not virtue at all. Cultivating various forms of "what should be," which are called virtue—like nonviolence—practicing these day after day until they become mechanical, has no meaning.

Virtue, surely, is something from moment to moment, like beauty, like love—it is not something you have accumulated and from which you act. This is not just a verbal statement for acceptance or nonacceptance. There is disorder—not only in society but in ourselves, total disorder—but it is not that there is somewhere in us order and the rest of the field is in disorder; that is another duality and therefore contradiction, confusion and struggle. Where there is disorder there must be choice and conflict. It is only the mind that is confused that chooses, but for a mind that sees everything very clearly there is no choice. If I am confused, my actions will be confused.

A mind that sees things very clearly, without distortion, without a personal bias, has understood disorder and is free of it; such a mind is virtuous, orderly—not orderly according to the Communists, the Socialists or the Capitalists or any church, but orderly because it has understood the whole measure of disorder within itself. Order, inwardly, is akin to the absolute order of mathematics. Inwardly, the highest order is as an absolute; and it cannot come about through cultivation, not through practice, oppression, control, obedience and conformity. It is only a mind that is highly ordered that can be sensitive, intelligent.

One has to be aware of disorder within oneself, aware of the contradictions, the dualistic struggles, the opposing desires, aware of the ideological pursuits and their unreality.

21

One has to observe "that which is" without condemnation, without judgment, without any evaluation. I see the microphone is the microphone—not as something I like or dislike, considering it good or bad—I see it as it is. In the same way one has to see oneself as one is, not calling what one sees bad, good—evaluating (which does not mean doing what one likes). Virtue is order; one cannot have a blueprint of it; if one does, and if one follows it, one has become immoral, disorderly.

Questioner: Is order simply not disorder?

KRISHNAMURTI: No. We said that the understanding of what disorder is—understanding not verbally, not intellectually—is actually to be free of disorder, which is the conflict, the battle of duality. Out of that understanding comes order, which is a living thing. That which is alive you cannot put on a piece of paper and try to follow it—it is a movement.

Our minds are tortured, our minds are twisted, because we are making such tremendous efforts to live, to do, to act, to think. Effort in any form must be a distortion. The moment there is an effort to be aware, it is not awareness. I am aware as I enter this hall; I do not make an effort. I am aware of the size of the hall, the color of the curtains, the lights, the people, the color of what they wear—I am aware of it all, there is no effort. When attention is an effort it is inattention.

Questioner: Something takes me from inattention.

KRISHNAMURTI: Nothing takes you from inattention to attention. One is mostly inattentive. If you know you are inattentive and be attentive at the moment of knowing inattention you are attentive.

To look at something objectively, without any judgment, is fairly easy. Look at a tree, at a flower, or the cloud, or the light on the water, to look at it without any judgment or evaluation is fairly easy—because it does not touch us deeply. But to look at my wife, at my professor, without any evaluation, is almost impossible, because I have an image of that person. That image has been put together through a series of incidents over days, months and years —with their pleasure, pain, sexual delight and so on. It is through that image that I look at that person. See what happens: when I look at my wife or my neighbor—or the neighbor may be a thousand or ten thousand miles away —I look at her or him through the images I have built and through the images which propaganda has built. Have I any relationship?—is there any relationship between the husband and the wife when both of them have their images? The images have relationship—the memories of the experiences, the nagging, the bullying, the dominating, the pleasure, this and that—which have been accumulated for years. Through these memories, these images, I look and I say, "I know my wife," or she says she knows me. But is that so? I know merely the images; a living thing I cannot know—dead images are what I know.

To look clearly is to look without any image, without any symbol or word. Do it and you will see what great beauty there is.

Questioner: Can I look at myself that way?

KRISHNAMURTI: If you look at yourself with an image about yourself, you cannot learn. For instance, I discover in myself a deep-rooted hatred and I say, "How terrible, how ugly." When I say that, I prevent myself from looking. The verbal statement, the word, the symbol, prevents observation. To learn about myself there must be no word, no knowledge, no symbol, no image; then I am actively learning.

Questioner: Is it possible to observe all the time?

KRISHNAMURTI: I wonder why one asks such a question. Is it a form of greed? You say: "If I could do that my life would be different"—therefore you are greedy. Forget whether you can do it all the time—you will find out. Begin and see how extraordinarily difficult it is to be attentive.

Questioner: (*Inaudible on tape.*)

KRISHNAMURTI: Through the senses of my body there is visual sight; and there is also psychological sight; I see visually, why should I introduce the sight of psychological memories into what I am seeing?

All this is meditation. You cannot say there is all this and that meditation is at the end of it! All this is the way of living which is meditation and that is the beauty of it; beauty, not as in architecture, in the line and curve of a hill, of the setting sun or the moon, not in the word or in the poem, not in a statue or a painting—it is in a way of living, you can look at anything and there is beauty.

Is it possible for a mind that is twisted, broken, fragmentary, to see everything clearly and innocently? We are tortured human beings, there is no question about it, our minds have been tortured and are tortured—how can such a mind see things very clearly? To find that out—because we are learning, not stating things—to find that out one must go into the question of experience.

Every experience leaves a mark, a residue, a memory of pain or pleasure. The word "experience" means to go through something. But we never "go through" something so it leaves a mark. If you have a great experience, go through the greatness of it, completely, so that you are free of it, then it does not leave marks as memory.

Why is it that every experience that we have had leaves a remembrance, conscious or unconscious?—because it is this that prevents innocency. You cannot prevent experiences. If you prevent or resist experience, you build a wall around yourself, you isolate yourself; that is what most people do.

One must understand the nature and structure of experience. You see a sunset such as it was yesterday evening —lovely, the light, that rose-colored light on the water and the top of the trees bathed in marvelous light. You look at it, you enjoy it, there is a great delight and beauty, color and depth; a second later you say, "How beautiful it was." You describe it to somebody, you want it again, the beauty of it, the pleasure of it, the delight of it. You may be back tomorrow, at that time and hour and you may see the sun-

24

set again—but you will look at it with the memory of yesterday's. So the freshness is already affected by the memory of yesterday. In the same way, you may insult me, or flatter me, the insult and the flattery remain as marks of pain and pleasure. So I am accumulating, the mind is accumulating through experience, thickening, coarsening, becoming more and more heavy with thousands of experiences. That is a fact. Now, can I when you insult me, listen with attention and consider your insult, not react to it immediately, but consider it? When you say I am a fool, you may be right, I may be a fool, probably I am. Or when you flatter me, I also watch. Then the insult and the flattery leave no mark. The mind is alert, watchful, whether of your insult or flattery, of the sunset and the beauty of so many things. The mind is all the time alert and therefore all the time free—though receiving a thousand experiences.

Questioner: If somebody insults you and you really listen to what they are saying, after you have heard it . . . well, are they right or are they wrong?

KRISHNAMURTI: No, you can see it instantly, the mind being free from the past, the psychological accumulation of knowledge and experience. You can be innocent.

Questioner: Then it must be attentive.

KRISHNAMURTI: Of course. And in that there is great joy. In the other there is not; there the mind is twisted, tortured by experience, and therefore can never be innocent, fresh, young, alive.

There is the whole question of love. Have you ever considered what it is? Is love thought or its product? Can love be cultivated by thought—become a habit? Is love pleasure? Love as we know it is essentially the pursuit of pleasure. And if love is pleasure, then love is also fear—no?

What is pleasure? We are not denying pleasure; we are not saying you must not have pleasure; that would be absurd. What is pleasure? You saw that sunset yesterday evening; at the moment of perception there was neither pleasure nor pain, there was only an immediate contact with that reality. But a few minutes later you began to think about it; what a delightful thing that was. It is the same with sex. You think about it by building images and pictures; thinking about it gives you pleasure. In the same way, thinking about the loss of that pleasure, you have fear —thinking about not having a job tomorrow, being lonely, not being loved, not being capable of self-expression and so on. This machinery of "thinking about it" causes both pleasure and fear.

Is love to be cultivated as you would cultivate a plant? Is love to be cultivated by thought?—knowing that thought breeds pleasure and fear. One has to learn what love is, *learn*, not accumulate what others have said about love— what horror! One has to learn, one has to observe. Love is not to be cultivated by thought; love is something entirely different.

From the sensitivity and intelligence, from the order born when the mind understands how this disorder comes into being and is free of it, from the discipline which comes in the understanding of disorder, one comes upon this thing called love—which the politicians, the priests, the husband, the wife, have destroyed.

To understand love is to understand death. If one does not die to the past, how can one love? If I do not die to the *image* of myself and to the *image* of my wife, how can I love?

All this is the marvel of meditation and the beauty of it. In all this, one comes upon something: the quality of mind which is religious and silent. Religion is not organized belief, with its gods, with its priests. Religion is a state of mind, a free mind, an innocent mind and therefore a completely silent mind—such a mind has no limit.

Questioner: What happens to people who do not have this type of mind?

KRISHNAMURTI: Why do we say: "If people do not have it"? Who are "the people"? If I do not have it—that is all. If I do not have such a sharp, clear mind, what am I to do? Is not that the question? Our minds are confused, are they not? We live in confusion. What should one do? If I am

26

stupid, Sir, it is no good trying to polish stupidity, trying to become clever. First I must know I am stupid, that I am dull. The very awareness of my dullness is to be free of that dullness. To say "I am a fool," not verbally but actually say "Well, I am a fool," then you are already watchful, you are no longer a fool. But if you resist what you are, then your dullness becomes more and more.

In this world the apogee of intellect is to be very clever, very smart, very complex, very erudite. I do not know why people carry erudition in their brains—why not leave it on the library shelf? The computers are very erudite. Erudition has nothing whatsoever to do with intelligence. To see things as they are, in ourselves, without bringing about conflict in perceiving what we are needs the tremendous simplicity of intelligence. I am a fool, I am a liar, I am angry and so on: I observe it, I learn about it, not relying on any authority, I do not resist it, I do not say "I must be different," it is just there.

Questioner: When I attempt to pay attention I realize that I cannot give attention.

KRISHNAMURTI: Is attention born of inattention?

Questioner: No: what produces it—how does it come?

KRISHNAMURTI: First of all, what is attention? When you attend, that is, when you give your mind, your heart, your nerves, your eyes, your ears, there is complete attention; it takes place, does it not? Total attention is that. When there is no resistance, when there is no censor, no evaluating movement, then there is attention—you have got it.

Questioner: But it seems so seldom.

KRISHNAMURTI: Ah!—we are back again. "This happens so seldom!" I am just pointing out something, which is: most of us are inattentive. Now, next time you are conscious of inattention, you are attentive, are you not? So be conscious of inattention. Through negation you come to the positive. Through understanding inattention, attention comes.

FOUR TALKS AT THE UNIVERSITY OF CALIFORNIA AT BERKELEY

1

What is important is to listen, not only to the speaker, but also to our reactions to what is being said, because the speaker is not going to deal with any particular philosophy, he is not in any way representing India, or any of its philosophies. We are concerned with human problems, not with philosophies and beliefs. We are concerned with human sorrow, the sorrow that most of us have, the anxiety, the fear, the hopes and despairs, and the great disorder that exists throughout the world. With that we are concerned as human beings, because we are responsible for this colossal chaos in the world, we are responsible for the disorder, for the war that is going on in Vietnam, we are responsible for the riots. As human beings living in this world in different countries and societies we are actually responsible for everything that is going on. I don't think we realize how serious this responsibility is. Some of us may feel it and so we want to do something, join a particular group, or a particular sect or belief, and devote all our lives to that ideology, that particular action. But that does not solve the problem nor absolve our particular responsibility.

So we must be concerned first with understanding what the problem is, not what to do; that will come later.

Most of us want to do something, we want to commit ourselves to a particular course of action and unfortunately that leads to more chaos, more confusion, more brutality.

We must, I think, look at the problem as a whole, not at a particular part of that problem, not at a segment or a fragment of it, but at the whole problem of living, which includes going to the office, the family, love, sex, conflict, ambition and the understanding of what death is; and also if there is something called God, or truth, or whatever name one might give it. We must understand the totality of this problem. That is going to be our difficulty, because we are so used to act and react to a given problem and not to see that all human problems are interrelated. So it seems that to bring about a complete psychological revolution is far more important than an economic or social revolution —upsetting a particular establishment, either in this country or in France, or in India—because the problems are much deeper, much more profound than merely becoming an activist, or joining a particular group, or withdrawing into a monastery to meditate, learning Zen or Yoga.

Before you ask the speaker questions, first let us look at the problem. This is not something that you come to listen to for an hour or so and then forget about. We are concerned with human problems. You and I have to work very hard this evening. You are not here merely to gather a few ideas with which you agree, or disagree, or to try to find out what the speaker has to say. You will find that he has to say very little, because both of us are going to examine the problems, not taking any decision, but understanding the problems; and that very understanding will bring about its own action. So please—if I may suggest—listen, neither agreeing nor disagreeing, not coming to any conclusion. Listen without any prejudice, without preconceived ideas, because for centuries we have played this kind of game with words, with ideas, with ideologies and they have led no-where—we still suffer, we are still in turmoil, we are still seeking a bliss that is not pleasure.

As we said, we are concerned with the whole problem of living, not one particular part or portion of it. So first let us see what our problems are, not how to solve them, not what to do about them, because the moment we understand what the problem is, that very understanding brings about its own action; I think that is very important to realize. Most of us look at problems with a conclusion, with an assumption; we are not free to look, we are not free to observe what actually is. When we are free to look, to explore what the problem is, then out of that observation, that exploration, there comes understanding. And that understanding itself is action, not a conclusion leading to action. We will go into it and perhaps we will understand each other as we go along.

You know, wherever one goes in the world, human beings are more or less the same. Their manners, behavior and outward pattern of action may differ, but psychologically, inwardly, their problems are the same. Man throughout the world is confused, that is the first thing one observes. Uncertain, insecure, he is groping, searching, asking, looking for a way out of this chaos. So he goes to teachers, to yogis, to gurus, to philosophers; he is looking everywhere for an answer and probably that is why most of you are here, because we want to find a way out of this trap in which we are caught, without realizing that we, as human beings, have made this trap—it is of our own making and nobody else's. The society in which we live is the result of our psychological state. The society *is* ourselves, the world is ourselves, the world is not different from us. What we are we have made the world because we are confused, we are ambitious, we are greedy, seeking power, position, prestige. We are aggressive, brutal, competitive, and we build a society which is equally competitive, brutal and violent. It seems to me that our responsibility is to understand ourselves first, because *we are* the world. This is not an egotistic, limited point of view, as you will see when you begin to go into these problems.

What is the problem when we observe the actual world around us and in us? Is it an economic problem, a racial problem, black against white, the communists against the capitalists, one religion opposed to another religion—is that the problem? Or is the problem much deeper, more profound, a psychological problem? Surely it is not merely an outward, but much more an inward problem.

As we said, man by nature is aggressive, brutal, competitive, dominating; you can see this in yourself if you observe yourself. And if I may suggest, what we are going to talk over together this evening and during the next three evenings, is not a series of ideas to which you listen. What the speaker has to say is a psychological fact which you can observe in yourself. So if you will, use the speaker to observe yourself. Use the speaker as a mirror in which you see yourself without any distortion and thereby learn what you actually are.

So what is important is to learn about yourself, not according to any specialist, but to learn by actually observing yourself. And there you will find that you are the world: the hatreds, the nationalist, the religious separatist, the man who believes in certain things and disbelieves in others, the man who is afraid and so on. By observing the problem we are going to learn about ourselves. What is the problem that confronts each one of us? Is it a separate, particular problem, an economic or a racial problem, or the problem of some particular fear or neurosis, of believing or disbelieving in God, or of belonging to a particular sect— religious, political or otherwise? Do you look at the problem of living as a whole, or take a particular problem and give all your life to it, all your energy and thought? Do we take life as a whole? Life includes our conditioning brought about by economic pressures, by religious beliefs and dogmas, by national divisions, by racial prejudices. Life is this fear, this anxiety, this uncertainty, this torture, this travail. Life also includes love, pleasure, sex, death, and the question which man has been asking everlastingly, which is: Is there a reality, a something "beyond the hills," something which can be found through meditation? Man has always been asking this question and we cannot merely brush it aside as having no validity because we are only concerned with living from day to day; we want to know if there is an eternal thing, a timeless reality. All this is the problem, there is not one particular problem. When you observe this, you will find that all problems are interrelated. If you understand one problem completely, then you have understood all the problems.

As human beings, looking at this map of life, one of our major problems is fear. Not a particular fear, but *fear*: fear of living, fear of dying, fear of not being able to fulfill, of failure, fear of being dominated, suppressed, fear of insecurity, of death, of loneliness, fear of not being loved. Where there is fear, there is aggression. When one is afraid one becomes very active, not only to escape from fear but that fear brings about an aggressive activity. You can observe this in yourself if you care to. Fear is one of the major problems in life. How is it to be solved? Can man be free of fear forever, not only at the conscious level but also at the hidden, secret levels of his mind? Is that fear to be resolved through analysis? Is that fear to be wiped away by escaping? So this is the question: How is a mind that is afraid of living, afraid of the past, of the present, of the future, how is such a mind to be completely free of fear? Will it be free of it gradually, bit by bit—will it take time? And if you take time—many days, many years—you will get old and fear will still continue.

So how is the mind to be free of fear, not only of physical fear, but also of the structure of fear in the psyche, of psychological fears? You understand my question? Is fear to be dissolved completely, freed instantly, or is fear to be gradually understood and resolved little by little? That is the first question. Can the mind, which has been conditioned to think that it can gradually resolve fear, by taking time, through analysis, through introspective observation, gradually become free of fear? That is the traditional way. It is like those people who, being violent, have the ideology of nonviolence. They say, "We will gradually come to a state of nonviolence when the mind will not be violent at all." That will take time, perhaps ten years, perhaps a whole life-time, and in the meantime you are violent, you are sowing the seeds of violence. So there must be a way

—please do listen to this—there must be a way to completely end violence immediately; not through time, not through analysis, otherwise we are doomed as human beings to be violent for the rest of our lives. In the same way, can fear be ended completely? Can the mind be freed wholly from fear? Not at the end of one's life but now?

I do not know if you have ever asked such a question of yourself. And if you have, probably you have said, "It cannot be done" or "I don't know how to do it." And so you live with fear, you live with violence and you cultivate either courage or resistance or suppression or escape, or pursue an ideology of nonviolence. All ideologies are stupid because when you are pursuing an ideology, an ideal, you are escaping from "what is," and when you are escaping you cannot possibly understand "what is." So the first thing in understanding fear is *not* to escape, and that is one of the most difficult things. Not trying to escape through analysis, which takes time, or through drink, or by going to church, or various other kinds of activities. It is the same whether the escape is through drink, through a drug, through sex or through God. So can one cease to escape? That is the first problem in understanding what fear is and in dissolving it and being free from it entirely.

You know, for most of us freedom is something we don't want. We want to be free from a particular thing, from the immediate pressures or from immediate demands, but freedom is something entirely different; freedom is not licentiousness, doing what you like—freedom demands tremendous discipline, not the discipline of the soldier, not the discipline of suppression, of conformity. The word "discipline" means "to learn"; the root meaning of that word is "to learn." And to learn about something—it doesn't matter what—demands discipline, the very learning is discipline; not, you discipline yourself first, and then learn. The very act of learning *is* discipline, which brings about freedom from all suppression, from all imitation. So can you be free of fear, from which springs violence, from which spring all these divisions, religious and national, such as "my family" and "your family"?

Fear, when one knows it, is a dreadful thing. It makes everything go dark, there is no clarity, and a mind that is afraid cannot see what life is, what the real problems are. So the first thing, it seems to me, is to ask ourselves whether one can actually be free of fear, both physically and inwardly. When you meet a physical danger you react, and that is intelligence; it is not fear, otherwise you would destroy yourself. But when there are psychological fears—fear of tomorrow, fear of what one has done, fear of the present—intelligence does not operate. If one goes into it psychologically, inwardly, one will find for oneself that our whole social structure is based on the pleasure principle, because most of us are seeking pleasure and where there is the pursuit of pleasure there is also fear. Fear goes with pleasure. This is fairly obvious if you examine it.

How is the mind to be free of fear so completely that it sees everything very clearly? We are going to find out whether the mind is capable of freeing itself from fear altogether. You understand the question? We have accepted fear and lived with it, as we have accepted violence and war as the way of life. We have had thousands and thousands of wars and we are everlastingly talking about peace; but the way we live our *daily* life is war, a battlefield, a conflict. And we accept that as being inevitable. We have never asked ourselves whether we can live a life of complete peace, which means without conflict of any kind. Conflict exists because there is contradiction in ourselves. That is fairly simple. In ourselves there are different contradictory desires, opposing demands, and this brings conflict. We have accepted all these things as inevitable, as part of our existence; we have never questioned them.

One must be free of all belief, which means of all fear, to find out if there is such a thing as reality, a timeless state. To find that out there must be freedom—freedom from fear, freedom from greed, envy, ambition, competition, brutality; only then is the mind clear, without any complication, without any conflict. It is only such a mind that is still and it is only the still mind that can find out if there is such a thing as the eternal, the nameless. But you cannot come to that stillness through any practice, through any discipline. That stillness comes only when there is freedom—freedom from all this anxiety, fear, brutality, violence, jealousy. So can the mind be free—not eventually, not in ten or fifty years, but immediately?

I wonder, if you ask that question of yourself, what your answer will be? Whether you will say that it is possible, or not? If you say it is impossible, then you have blocked yourself, then you can't proceed further; and if you say it is possible, that also has its danger. You can only examine the possible if you know what is the impossible—right? We are asking ourselves a tremendous question, which is: "Can the mind, which throughout centuries has been conditioned politically, economically, by the climate, by the church, by various influences, can such a mind change immediately?" Or must it have time, endless days of analysis, of probing, exploring, searching? It is one of our conditionings that we accept time, an interval in which a revolution, a mutation, can take place. We need to change completely, *that* is the greatest revolution—not throwing bombs and killing each other. The greatest revolution is whether the mind can transform itself immediately and be entirely different tomorrow. Perhaps you will say such a thing is not possible. If you actually face the question without any escape and have come to that point when you say it is impossible, then you will find out what is possible; but you cannot put that question "What is possible?" without understanding what is impossible. Are we meeting each other?

So we are asking whether a mind that is afraid, that has been conditioned to be violent, to be aggressive, can transform itself immediately. And you can only ask that question (please follow this a little) when you understand the impossibility and the futility of analysis. Analysis implies

36

the analyzer, the one who analyzes, whether it be a professional analyst or yourself analyzing yourself. When you analyze yourself there are several things involved. First, whether the analyzer is different from the thing he analyzes. Is he different? Obviously, when you observe, the analyzer is the analyzed. There is no difference between the analyzer and the thing he is going to analyze. We miss that point, therefore we begin to analyze. I say "I am angry, I am jealous," and I begin to analyze why I am jealous, what are the causes of this jealousy, anger, brutality; but the analyzer is part of the thing he is analyzing. The observer is the observed and as one sees that, sees the futility of it, one will never analyze again. It is very important to understand this, to really see the truth of this—not verbally: verbal understanding is not understanding at all, it is like hearing a lot of words and saying, "Yes, I understand the words." To actually see that the analyzer, the observer, is the observed, is a tremendous fact, a tremendous reality; in that there is no division between the analyzer and the thing analyzed and therefore no conflict. Conflict exists only when the analyzer is different from the thing he analyzes; in that division there is conflict. Are you following this? Perhaps you will ask questions afterwards.

Our life is a conflict, a battlefield, but a mind that is free has no conflict and to be free of conflict is to observe the fact of the observer, the analyzer, the thinker. There is fear and the observer says "I am afraid"—please do follow this a little bit, you will see the beauty of it—so there is a division between the observer and the thing observed. Then the observer acts and says, "I must be different," "Fear must come to an end," he seeks the cause of the fear and so on; but the observer *is* the observed, the analyzer *is* the analyzed. When he realizes that nonverbally, the fact of fear undergoes a complete change.

Sirs, look, it is not mysterious. You are afraid, you are violent, you dominate, or you are dominated. Let's take something much simpler. You are jealous, envious. Is the observer different from that feeling which he calls jealousy?

37

If he is different, then he can act upon jealousy and that action becomes a conflict. If the entity that feels jealousy is the same as jealousy, then what can he do? I am jealous; as long as jealousy is different from "me" I am in a state of conflict, but if jealousy *is me*, not different from me, then what am I to do? I don't accept it, I say "I am jealous." That is a fact. I don't evade it, I don't run away from it, I don't try to suppress it. Whatever I do is still a form of jealousy. Therefore what happens? Inaction is total action. Inaction with regard to jealousy on the part of the observer as the observed, is the cessation of jealousy. Are you getting this? Are we communicating with each other?

Audience: Yes.

KRISHNAMURTI: Go easy, don't say "Yes." It is quite difficult. (*Laughter*) Because if you really understand this you are free of jealousy, you will never again be jealous. That is why it is very important to understand the whole of this conflict, this struggle that is going on inwardly, which expresses itself outwardly as violence. So can the mind be completely free of envy, which is jealousy? It can be free only when there is the realization that the observer is the observed and therefore there is no division. You understand? Look, Sirs, there is conflict in what we call relationship, between persons, between neighbors and so on. All relationship as it is now, is conflict—right? I think that is fairly obvious. Our relationships between each other, between human beings throughout the world, are based on an image which we have built about ourselves or about another. The husband builds an image about the wife and the wife builds an image about the husband—the image of pleasure, pain, insult, nagging, domination, jealousy, irritability, whatever it is. Gradually through many years an image has been built about the wife, or about the husband. The two images have relationship. Relationship means actual contact. To be related means to be in touch with something and you cannot be related to another if you have an image about him—obviously. So is it possible to live without an image and yet be related? Relationship brings conflict because we are *not* related; our relationship is between the images. Is it possible for a mind to be free of all image making? You understand the question?

I'll show you how it is possible. Don't accept it verbally but do it, then you will see what relationship actually means. It is the most extraordinary thing to be related. Then there is no pain, no conflict. What is the machinery that builds these images, about the President, or your wife, or your neighbor, or about God, or whatever it is? What is the structure and the nature of this image which we have about ourselves or about another? If I were married—which I am not—I would build an image about my wife: what she has said, what she has done, the pleasures she has given me sexually or otherwise, the fears, the domination, the nagging, all that. Gradually, day after day, I have built an image about her and she has built an image about me. This is a fact, not a supposition, and now I am asking myself whether I can be free of these images. You can only be free of the image when whatever is said—whether in anger, or in jealousy, in irritation, in flattery, or as an insult —you are completely aware at the moment of it being said, so that when you are flattered or insulted you see the truth of it and you are free of it. Which means that the mind must be completely attentive, so that it does not retain the particular experience of pleasure or pain which builds the image; that is, to be attentive at the moment when the wife or the husband says something pleasant or unpleasant. That attention, that choiceless awareness, gives freedom to look, to see the truth or the falseness of what is being said; then the mind no longer records it as memory. I do not know if you have ever tried it—probably you have not. The mind becomes extraordinarily active, alert, sensitive; then relationship, which is really one of the major problems of life, has quite a different meaning. Then relationship is the beauty of love without the image. However much one may say "I love you," love is not there. Love is something entirely different, love is not pleasure, love is not desire. To understand love one must understand pleasure and pleasure goes with fear, with pain—you cannot have one without the other.

So those are our problems. Those are the problems of every human being whether he lives in an affluent or primitive society. Man is suffering, man is in travail, and our problem, our question, is: whether the mind can transform itself completely, totally and thereby bring about a deep, psychological revolution—which is the *only* revolution. Such a revolution can bring about a different society, a different relationship, a different way of living.

Would you like to ask any questions? You know it is one of the most difficult things to ask questions. We have got a thousand questions we must ask; we must doubt everything. We mustn't obey or accept anything; we must find out for ourselves, we must see the truth for ourselves and not through another. And to see that truth one must be completely free. One must ask the right question to find the right answer, because if you ask the wrong questions you will inevitably receive wrong answers. So to ask the right question is one of the most difficult things—which doesn't mean the speaker is preventing you from asking questions. You must ask a question deeply, with great seriousness, because life is dreadfully serious. To ask such a question means that you have already explored your mind, already gone into yourself very deeply. So only the intelligent, self-knowing mind can ask the right question and in the very asking of it is the answering of it. Please don't laugh. This is most serious, because you always look to another to tell you what to do. We always want to light our lamp in the light of another. We are never a light to ourselves: to be a light to ourselves we must be free of all tradition, all authority, including that of the speaker, so that our own minds can look and observe and learn. To learn is one of the most difficult things. So to ask a question is fairly easy, but to ask the right question and to receive the right answer is something quite different.

Now, Sir, what is the question? (*Laughter*)

Questioner: *I came here tonight with a prepared question, which I gave up in the course of your talk because I began to see some of what you are getting at. I was going to ask you about Gandhi. I was going to ask your opinion, but now I have another question.*

Questioner: It may seem hard to some of the audience . . .

KRISHNAMURTI: Ask anything you like, Sir.

Questioner: When the equipment wasn't working properly and the people at the back couldn't hear, it seemed to me that a man of your experience would have known what to do in those circumstances. One wondered, were you feeling some residual fear yourself?

KRISHNAMURTI: He is asking, when the loudspeakers didn't function was I afraid? Why should I be afraid? It was a fault of the machinery and why should I be concerned about myself? I am afraid there was no fear. (*Laughter*) You see, Sir, the gentleman asked, "Would you offer an opinion about Gandhi?" or about X Y Z. Only fools offer opinions. Why should one have an opinion about another? Is is such a waste of time and energy. Why should one clutter up one's brain, one's mind, with opinions, judgments, conclusions? They prevent clarity and that clarity is denied when the mind observes with a conclusion.

Questioner: Our mind is clean, our mind is not involved in thought when it is perceiving only. It feels inside what is going on, it feels fear, or not, in another person, inside the person, without thinking what he is doing, what's going on.

KRISHNAMURTI: The questioner is saying—if I understand it rightly—"What is the mind, what is this mind that understands?" Is it thought that understands? Is that the question, Sir?

Questioner: Yes.

KRISHNAMURTI: We'll explore it, you will see it. When one says that one understands something, what is the state of the mind that says "I understand"? The word "understanding" can be used in two different ways. Either I understand verbally what you are saying, that is I hear the words and

41

I understand the meaning of the words, because you and I both speak English, use certain words which have a certain meaning and we say we understand those words. When understanding actually takes place—which is action in which there is feeling—there is attention, everything is involved when you say "I understood something very clearly." What is that state of mind that says "I have understood"?

Questioner: Total awareness.

KRISHNAMURTI: Now go into it a little bit more, Sirs. Doesn't awareness, doesn't understanding take place when the mind is not drawing a conclusion, has no opinion, when the mind is attentively listening, and then it says "I have understood"? We are asking what is the state of that mind which says "I have understood" and therefore acts immediately. Surely such a state of mind is complete silence in which there is no opinion, in which there is no judgment, no evaluation. It is actually listening out of silence. And it is only then that we understand something in which thought is not involved at all. We won't now go into what thought is and the whole process of thinking; that will need a lot of time and this is not the occasion. When we talk about understanding, surely it takes place only when the mind listens completely—the mind being your heart, your nerves, your ears—when you give your whole attention to it. I do not know if you have ever noticed that when you give total attention there is complete silence. And in that attention there is no frontier, there is no center, as the "me" who is aware or attentive. That attention, that silence, is a state of meditation. We can't go into what is implied by that word and how to come upon it, but we will go into it if we have time during the coming evenings.

So when you are listening to somebody, completely, attentively, then you are listening not only to the words, but also to the feeling of what is being conveyed, to the whole of it, not part of it.

Questioner: I find certain very serious contradictions in what you have said. I think that to begin with you said that only fools give opinions, that it is stupid.

KRISHNAMURTI: The gentleman says that I am giving opinions, evaluations, which contradict what I am saying. Have I given an opinion, a conclusion, a judgment? I have only said: look at the facts. It is not my fact or your fact, but the fact that man is violent. That's not an opinion, that's a fact. Man is a frightened animal, that's a fact. Man is jealous, man lives in conflict, his life is a battlefield and so on. These are not opinions, not judgments, this is actually what is going on inwardly in each one of us. How you translate it, what you do about it and whether you bring to it certain prejudices and conclusions, that is offering opinions. But we are only concerned with facts.

Questioner: I have a question here which I must ask. What is the basis of learning, which you say is difficult? You find yourself engaged in a specific task which is difficult. What is the basis for an action if you dispense with will and faith. How do you endure?

KRISHNAMURTI: I think I have understood. The questioner says, "What is learning?" Is learning different from action? Right, Sir?

Questioner: No. The question is: Why do you choose life or death! It is a matter of life and death if you engage in this activity. Where do you find in yourself the reservoir of strength to do a specific task which allows you to stay alive?

KRISHNAMURTI: I understand. Where do you find the energy—I am putting it differently—where do you find the energy to live rightly? Right?

Questioner: Yes. You don't will a thing, it comes by itself, if you do it with an undivided self.

KRISHNAMURTI: That's right.

Questioner: (Inaudible)

KRISHNAMURTI: I understand, Sir. That's just it. How do you live without will—right?—without contradiction, without the opposites? How do you live without conflict at all and at the same time act?

Questioner: Yes. You can choose to die.

KRISHNAMURTI: You can't choose to die, you have to live but—

Questioner: The question is how!

KRISHNAMURTI: Wait, Sir. The questioner says, "What is the method, what is the system I can learn which will help me to live without contradiction, to live actively, in a state of constant learning?" Is that the question?

First of all, what do we mean by learning? I am not offering an opinion, I am looking at the fact. Is learning a process of accumulation of knowledge? From that knowledge I act; that is, I have stored up experiences, memories, and from that I act. Or is learning a constant process without accumulation and therefore learning is acting? Go slowly. We'll go into it. It is not that I first learn and then act according to what I have learned, but learning is acting; the learning is not separate from acting. One is going to learn about fear, or about what to do, how to live. But if you have a system that tells you how to live, or a method that says, "Live this way," then you are conforming to the method which is established by somebody else. Therefore you are not learning, you are conforming and acting according to a pattern, which is not action at all, it is just imitation. So if you learn what are the implications of methods, or of systems, then you will put away methods and systems; then you are learning about what you are doing and the very learning about life is the activity of life—right? Have I made it clear? Living, learning and acting are not three separate things, they are indivisible.

Questioner: I did not get the point why it is detrimental for oneself to analyze; it's a difficult point.

KRISHNAMURTI: Aren't you tired after an hour and a half?

44

Questioner: Not at all.

KRISHNAMURTI: Not at all? Why not? (*Laughter*) Wait a minute, Sir. Why not? If you had been listening attentively —I am not criticizing you—you'd be tired, wouldn't you?

Questioner: I don't think so.

KRISHNAMURTI: Sir, the speaker has been working and to keep up with him you have to work too. It is not "he speaks" and "you listen" but we are taking the journey together, learning about ourselves, about the world, about what is happening in relationship with the world. And to learn about all this, obviously your mind must be tired after a long day's work and sitting here. You *must* be tired! But it doesn't matter, I'll go into this question and after that we'll stop.

The speaker said, that in the process of analysis several things are implied—time, for one thing. Obviously, to analyze implies spending day after day doing it. Secondly, the analyzer must analyze very, very carefully, otherwise he will go wrong. In order to analyze correctly he must be free from prejudice, from conclusions, from fear. If in the process any distortion takes place, that analysis will only create further limitations. And we also explained that the analyzer is not different from the thing he analyzes. When you understand all this, not just one part of it—the time, the process of analysis, the decisions, the conclusions which will prevent you from proceeding further with a clear analysis, and seeing that the analyzer is the analyzed— when you see the totality of this you will never analyze again. When you don't analyze, then you see things directly because the problem becomes intense, urgent. It's like a man who has an ideology of nonviolence and is therefore concerned with how to become nonviolent, but not how to be free, now, from all violence. We are concerned with freedom from violence *now*, not tomorrow.

When one observes this whole process of analysis— which has become the fashion—and sees what is implied in it, not only verbally but deeply, then one rejects it.

When you deny something false you are free to look; then you see what truth is. But you must first deny what is false.

2

Considering the chaos and disorder in the world—both outwardly and inwardly—seeing all this misery, starvation, war, hatred, brutality—many of us must have asked what one can do. As a human being confronted with this confusion, what can I or you do? When we put that question, we feel we must be committed to some kind of political or sociological action, or some kind of religious search and discovery. One feels one must be committed, and throughout the world this desire to be committed has become very important. Either one is an activist, or one withdraws from this social chaos and pursues a vision. I think it is far more important not to be committed at all, but to be totally involved in the whole structure and nature of life. When you commit yourself, you are committed to a part and therefore the part becomes important and that creates division. Whereas, when one is involved completely, totally, with the whole problem of living, action is entirely different. Then action is not only inward, but also outward; it is in relationship with the whole problem of life. To be involved implies total relationship with every problem, with every thought and feeling of the human mind. And when one is so completely involved in life and not committed to any particular part or fragment of it, then one has to see what one can actually do as a human being.

For most of us, action is derived from an ideology. First we have an idea about what we should do, the idea being an ideology, a concept, a formula. Having formulated what we should do, we act according to that ideology. So there is always a division, and hence a conflict between action and what you have formulated that action should be. And as most of one's life is a series of conflicts, struggles, one inevitably asks oneself whether one can live in this world being completely involved with it, not in some isolated monastery.

Inevitably this brings about another question, which is: What is relationship? Because it is in that that we are involved—man in relationship with another man—that is the whole of life. If there were no relationship at all, if one actually lived completely in isolation, life would cease. Life is a movement in relationship. To understand that relationship and to end the conflict in that relationship is our entire problem. It is to see whether man can live at peace not only within himself, but also outwardly. Because then behavior is righteous and we are concerned with behavior, which is action. You might ask, "What can one individual, one human being do, confronted with this immense problem of life with its confusion, wars, hatred, agony, suffering?" What can one human being do to bring about a change, a revolution, a radical state, a new way of looking, living? I think that is a wrong question, to say, "What can I do to affect this total confusion and disorder." If you put that question, "What can I do, confronted with this disorder," then you have already answered it; you can't do anything. Therefore it is a wrong question. But if you are concerned, not with what you can do confronted with this enormity of misery, but with how you can live a totally different life, then you will find that your relationship with man, with the whole community, with the world, undergoes a change. Because after all, you and I as human beings, we are the entire world—I'm not saying this rhetorically, but actually: I and you are the entire world. What one thinks, what one feels, the agony, the suffering, the ambition, the envy, the extraordinary confusion one is in, that is the world. There must be a change in the world, a radical revolution, one can't live as one is living, a bourgeois life, a life of superficiality, a life of shoddy existence from day to day, indifferent to what is happening. If you and I, as human beings, can change totally, then whatever we do will be righteous. Then we will not bring about a conflict within ourselves and therefore outwardly. So that is the problem. That is what the speaker wants to talk over with you this evening. Because as we said, how one conducts one's life, what one does in daily life—not at a moment of great crisis but actually every day—is of the highest importance. Relationship *is* life, and this relationship is a constant movement, a constant change.

So our question is: How am I, or you, to change so fundamentally, that tomorrow morning you wake up as a different human being meeting any problem that arises, resolving it instantly and not carrying it over as a burden, so that there is great love in your heart and you see the beauty of the hills and the light on the water? To bring about this change, obviously one must understand oneself, because self-knowledge, not theoretically but actually, whatever you are, is of the highest importance.

You know, when one is confronted with all these problems, one is deeply moved; not by words, not by the description, because the word is not the thing, the description is not the described. When one observes oneself as one actually is, then either one is moved to despair because one considers oneself as hopeless, ugly, miserable; or one looks at oneself without any judgment. And to look at oneself without any judgment is of the greatest importance, because that is the only way you can understand yourself and know about yourself. And in observing oneself objectively—which is not a process of self-centeredness, or self-isolation, or cutting oneself off from the whole of mankind or from another human being—one realizes how terribly one is conditioned: by the economic pressures, by the culture in which one has lived, by the climate, by the food one eats, by the propaganda of the so-called religious organizations or by the communists. This conditioning is not superficial but it goes down very deeply and so one asks whether one can ever be free of it, because if one is not free, then one is a slave, then one lives in incessant conflict and battle, which has become the accepted way of life.

I hope you are listening to the speaker, not merely to the

words but using the words as a mirror to observe yourself. Then communication between the speaker and yourself becomes entirely different, then we are dealing with facts and not suppositions, or opinions, or judgments, then we are both concerned with this problem of how the mind can be unconditioned, changed completely. As we said, this understanding of oneself is only possible by becoming aware of our relationships. In relationship alone can one observe oneself; there all the reactions, all the conditionings are exposed. So in relationship one becomes aware of the actual state of oneself. And as one observes, one becomes aware of this immense problem of fear.

One sees the mind is always demanding to be certain, to be secure, to be safe. A mind that is safe, secure, is a bourgeois mind, a shoddy mind. Yet that is what all of us want: to be completely safe. And psychologically there is no such thing. See what takes place outwardly—it's quite interesting if you observe it—each person wants to be safe, secure. And yet psychologically he does everything to bring about his own destruction. You can see this. As long as there are nationalities with their sovereign governments, with their armies and navies and so on, there must be war. And yet psychologically we are conditioned to accept that we are a particular group, a particular nation, belonging to a particular ideology, or religion. I do not know if you have ever observed what mischief the religious organizations have done in the world, how they have divided man. You are a Catholic, I am a Protestant. To us the label is much more important than the actual state of affection, love, kindliness. Nations have divided us, nationalities have divided us. One can observe this division, which is our conditioning and which brings about fear.

So we are going to go into the question of what to do with fear. Unless we resolve this fear we live in darkness, we live in violence. A man who is not afraid is not aggressive, a man who has no sense of fear of any kind is really a free, a peaceful man. As human beings we must resolve this problem, because if we cannot, we cannot possibly live righteously. Unless one understands behavior, conduct in which is involved virtue—you may spit on that word—and unless one is totally free of fear, the mind can never discover what truth is, what bliss is, and if there is such a thing as a timeless state. When there is fear you want to escape, and that escape is quite absurd, immature. So we have this problem of fear. Can the mind be free of it entirely, both at the conscious as well as at the so-called unconscious, deeper levels of the mind? That is what we are going to talk over this evening, because without understanding this question of fear and resolving it, the mind can never be free. And it is only in freedom that you can explore, discover. It is very important, it is essential, that the mind be free of fear. So shall we go into it?

Now first of all do please bear in mind that the description is not the described, so don't be caught by the description, by the words. The word, the description, is merely a means of communicating. But if you are held by the word you cannot go very far. One has to be aware not only of the meaning of the word, but also one has to realize that the word is not actually the thing. So what is fear? I hope we are going to do it together. Please don't just listen and disregard it; be involved, entirely live it. Because it is *your* fear, it's not mine. We are taking a journey together into this very complex problem of fear. If one doesn't understand it and become free of it, relationship is not possible: relationship remains conflict, travail, misery.

What is fear? One is afraid of the past, of the present, or of something that might happen tomorrow. Fear involves time. One is afraid of death; that is in the future. Or one is afraid of something that has happened. Or one is afraid of the pain one has had when one was ill. Please follow this closely. Fear implies time: one is afraid of something—of some pain that one has had and which might happen again. One is afraid of something that might take place tomorrow, in the future. Or one is afraid of the present. All that involves time. Psychologically speaking, if there were no yesterday, today and tomorrow, there would be no fear. Fear is not only of time but it is the product of thought. That is, in thinking about what happened yesterday—which was painful—I am thinking that it might happen again tomorrow. Thought produces this fear. Thought breeds fear: thinking about the pain, thinking about death, thinking about the frustrations, the fulfillments, what might happen, what should be, and so on. Thought produces fear and gives vitality to the continuance of fear. And thought, by thinking about what has given you pleasure yesterday, sustains that pleasure, gives it duration. So thought produces, sustains, nourishes, not only fear but also pleasure. Please observe it in yourself, see what actually goes on within you.

You have had a pleasurable or so-called enjoyable experience and you think about it. You want to repeat it, whether it is sex or any other experience. Thinking about that thing which has given a pleasurable moment, you want that pleasure repeated, continued. So thought is not only responsible for fear, but also for pleasure. One sees the truth of this, the actual fact that thought sustains pleasure and nourishes fear. Thought breeds both fear and pleasure; the two are not separate. Where there is the demand for pleasure, there must also be fear; the two are unavoidable because they are both the product of thought.

Please let's bear in mind that I am not persuading you of anything, I'm not making propaganda. God forbid! Because to make propaganda is to lie; if someone is trying to convince you of something, don't be convinced. We are dealing with something much more serious than being convinced, or with offering opinions and judgments. We are dealing with realities, with facts. And facts, which you observe, don't need an opinion. You haven't got to be told what the fact is, it is there, if you are capable of observing it.

So one sees that thought sustains and nourishes fear as well as pleasure. We want pleasure continued, we want more and more pleasure. The ultimate pleasure for man is to find out if there is a permanent state in heaven which is God; to him God is the highest form of pleasure. And if you observe, all social morality—which is really immoral—is based on pleasure and fear, reward and punishment.

Then one asks, when one sees this actual fact—not the description, not the word, but the thing described, the actual state of how thought brings this about: "Is it possible for thought to come to an end?" The question sounds rather crazy, but it is not. You saw a sunset yesterday, the hills were extraordinarily lit in the evening sun and there was a glory, a beauty that gave you great enjoyment. Can one enjoy it so completely that it comes to an end, so that thought doesn't carry it over to tomorrow? And can one face fear, if there is such a thing as fear? This is only possible when you understand the whole structure and nature of thought. So one asks, "What is thinking?"

For most of us thinking has become extraordinarily important. We never realize that thought is always old, thought is never new, thought can never be free. We were talking about freedom of thought, which is sheer nonsense, which means you may express what you want, say what you like; but thought in itself is never free, because thought is the response of memory. One can observe this for oneself. Thought is the response of memory, experience, knowledge. Knowledge, experience, memory, are always old and so thought is always old. Therefore thought can never see anything new. Can the mind look at the problem of fear without the interference of thought? Do you understand, Sirs?

I am afraid. There is fear of what one has done. Be completely aware of it without the interference of thought—and then is there fear? As we said, fear is brought about through time; time is thought. This is not philosophy, not some mystical experience; just observe it in yourself, you will see. One realizes thought must function objectively, efficiently, logically, healthily. When you go to the office, or whatever you do, thought must operate, otherwise you cannot do anything. But the moment thought breeds or sustains pleasure and fear, then thought becomes inefficient. Thought then breeds inefficiency in relationship and therefore causes conflict. So one asks whether there can be an ending of thought in one direction, and yet with thought functioning in its highest capacity. We are concerned with whether thought can be absent when the mind sees the sunset in all its beauty. It is only then that you see the beauty of the sunset, not when your mind is full of thoughts, problems, violence. That is, if you have observed it, at the moment of seeing the sunset thought is absent. You look at this extraordinary light on the mountain, it is a great delight and at that moment thought has no place in it at all. But the next moment thought says: "How marvelous that was, how beautiful, I wish I could paint it, I wish I could write a poem about it, I wish I could tell my friends what a lovely thing it is." Or thought says: "I would like to see that sunset again tomorrow." Then thought begins its mischief. Because thought then says: "Tomorrow I will have that pleasure again," and when you don't have it there is pain. This is very simple, and because of its very simplicity it gets lost. We all want to be terribly clever, we are all so sophisticated, intellectual, we read such a lot. The whole psychological history of mankind (not who was king and what kind of wars there were and all the absurdity of nationalities) is within oneself. When you can read that in yourself you have understood. Then you are a light to yourself, then there is no authority, then you are actually free.

So our question is: Can thought cease to interfere? And it is this interference that produces time. Do you understand? Take death. There is great beauty in what is involved in death, and it is not possible to understand that beauty if there is any form of fear. We are just showing how frightened we are of death, because it might happen in the future and it is inevitable. So thought thinks about it and shuts it out. Or thought thinks about the fear that you have had, the pain, the anxiety, and that it might be repeated. We are caught in the mischief made by thought. Yet one also realizes the extraordinary importance of thought. When you go to the office, when you do something technological, you must use thought and knowledge. Seeing the whole process of it from the beginning of this talk till now—seeing the whole of that—one asks, "Can thought be silent?" Can one look at the sunset and be completely involved in the beauty of that sunset, without thought bringing into it the question of pleasure? Please follow this. Then conduct becomes righteous. Conduct becomes virtuous only when thought does not cultivate what it considers to be virtue, which then becomes unholy and ugly. Virtue is not of time or of thought; which means virtue is not a product of pleasure or of fear. So now the question is: How is it possible to look at the sunset without thought weaving round it pleasure or pain? Can one look at this sunset with such attention, with such complete involvement in that beauty, so that when you have seen that sunset it is ended and not taken over by thought, as pleasure, for tomorrow?

Are we communicating with each other? Are we? (*Audience: Yes, yes.*) Good, I'm glad, but don't be so quick in answering "Yes." (*Laughter*) For this is quite a difficult problem. To watch the sunset without the interference of thought demands tremendous discipline; not the discipline of conformity, not the discipline of suppression or control. The word "discipline" means "to learn"—not to conform, not to obey—to learn about the whole process of thinking and its place. The negation of thought needs great observation. And to observe there must be freedom. In this freedom one knows the movement of thought, and then learning is active.

What do we mean by learning? When one goes to school or college one learns a great deal of information, perhaps not of great importance, but one learns. That becomes knowledge and from that knowledge we act, either in the technological field, or in the whole field of consciousness. So one must understand very deeply what that word "to learn" means. The word "to learn" obviously is an active present. There is learning all the time. But when that learning becomes a means to the accumulation of knowledge, then it is quite a different thing. That is, I have learned from past experience that fire burns. That is knowledge. I have learned it, therefore I don't go near the fire. I have ceased to learn. And most of us, having learned, act from there. Having gathered information about ourselves (or about another) this becomes knowledge; then that knowledge becomes almost static and from that we act. Therefore action is always old. So learning is something entirely different.

If one has listened this evening with attention, one has learned the nature of fear and pleasure; one has learned it and from that one acts. You see the difference, I hope. Learning implies a constant action. There is learning all the time. And the very act of learning is doing. The doing is not separate from learning. Whereas for most of us the doing is separate from the knowledge. That is, there is the ideology or the ideal, and according to that ideal we act, approximating the action only to that ideal. Therefore action is always old.

Learning, like seeing, is a great art. When you see a flower, what takes place? Do you see the flower actually, or do you see it through the image you have of that flower? The two things are entirely different. When you look at a flower, at a color, without naming it, without like or dislike, without any screen between you and the thing you see as a flower, without the word, without thought, then the flower has an extraordinary color and beauty. But when you look at the flower through botanical knowledge, when you say: "This is a rose," you have already conditioned your looking. Seeing and learning is quite an art, but you don't go to college to learn it. You can do it at home. You can look at a flower and find out how you look at it. If you are sensitive, alive, watching, then you will see that the space between you and the flower disappears and when that space disappears you see the thing so vitally, so strongly! In the same way when you observe yourself without that space (not as "the observer" and "the thing observed") then you will see there is no contradiction and therefore no conflict.

In seeing the structure of fear, one also sees the structure and nature of pleasure. The seeing is the learning about it and therefore the mind is not caught in the pursuit of pleasure. Then life has quite a different meaning. One lives —not in search of pleasure.

Wait a minute before you ask questions. I would like to ask you a question: What have you got out of this talk? Don't answer me, please. Find out whether you got words, descriptions, ideas, or if you got something that is true, that is irrevocable, indestructible, because you yourself have seen it. Then you are a light to yourself and therefore you will not light your candle at any other light; you are that light yourself. If that is a fact, not a hypocritical assumption, then a gathering of this kind has been worthwhile. Now, perhaps, would you like to ask questions?

As we said yesterday, you are asking questions to find out, not to show that you are more intelligent than the speaker. A person who compares is not intelligent; an intelligent man never compares. Either you ask a question because by asking you would reveal yourself, expose yourself to yourself and thereby learn, or you ask a question to trip up the speaker—which you are perfectly welcome to do. Or you ask a question to have a wider view, to open the door. So it depends on you what kind and what quality of question you are going to ask. Which doesn't mean, please, that the speaker does not want you to ask questions.

Questioner: What is one to do when one notices the sunset and at the same time thought is coming into it?

KRISHNAMURTI: What is one to do? Please understand the significance of the question. That is, you see the sunset, thought interferes with it, and then you say "What is one to do?" Who is the questioner who says "What is one to do?" Is it thought that says what am I to do? Do you understand the question? Let me put it this way. There is the sunset, the beauty of it, the extraordinary color, the feeling of it, the love of it; then thought comes along and I say to myself: "Here it is, what am I to do?" Do listen to it carefully, do go into it. Is it not thought also that says "What am I to do?" The "I" who says "What am I to do?" is the result of thought. So thought, seeing what is interfering with this beauty, says: "What am I to do?"

Don't do anything! (*Laughter*) If you *do* something, you bring conflict into it. But when you see the sunset and thought comes in, *be aware* of it. Be aware of the sunset and the thought that comes into it. Don't chase thought away. Be choicelessly aware of this whole thing: the sunset and thought coming into it. Then you will find, if you are so aware, without any desire to suppress thought, to struggle against the interference of thought, if you don't do any of those things then thought becomes quiet. Because it is thought itself that is saying "What am I to do?" That is one of the tricks of thought. Don't fall into the trap, but observe this whole structure of what is happening.

Questioner: We are conditioned how to look at the sunset, we are conditioned how we listen to you as the speaker. So through our conditioning we look at everything and listen to everything. How is one to be free of this conditioning?

KRISHNAMURTI: When are you aware of this conditioning, of any conditioning? Do please follow it a little bit. When are you aware that you are conditioned? Are you aware that you are conditioned as an American, as a Hindu, as a Catholic, Protestant, Communist, this and that? Are you aware that you are so conditioned, or are you aware of it because somebody has told you? If you are aware because someone has pointed out to you that you are conditioned, then that is one kind of awareness. But if you aware that you are conditioned without being told, then it has a different quality. If you are told that you are hungry, that is one thing; but if you are actually hungry that is another. Now find out which it is: whether you were told you are conditioned and therefore you realize it; or, because you are aware, because you are involved in this whole process of living, and because of that awareness you realize for yourself, without being told, that you are conditioned. Then that has a vitality, then it becomes a problem that you have to understand very deeply. One sees that one is conditioned, not because one is told. The obvious reaction to it is to throw away that conditioning, if you are intelligent. Becoming aware of a particular conditioning, you revolt against it, as the present generation is revolting—which is merely a reaction. Revolt against a conditioning forms another kind of conditioning. One becomes aware of one's conditioning as a Communist, a Protestant, a Democrat, or a Republican. What takes place when there is no reaction but only awareness of what this conditioning actually is? What takes place when you are choicelessly aware of this conditioning, which you have found for yourself? There is no reaction. Then you are learning about this conditioning, why it comes into being. Two thousand years of propaganda have made you believe in a particular form of religious dogma. You are aware of how the church through centuries upon centuries, through tradition, repetition, through various rituals and entertainments, has conditioned our minds. There has been the repetition day after day, month after month, from childhood on; we are baptized and all the rest of it. And another form of the same thing takes place in other countries like India, China and so on.

Now when you become aware of it, what happens? You see how quickly the mind is influenced. The mind being pliable, young, innocent, is conditioned as a Communist, Catholic, Protestant and so on. Why is it conditioned? Why is it so shaped by propaganda? Are you following this? Why are you persuaded by propaganda to buy certain things, to believe in certain things, why? Not only is there this constant pressure from the outside, but also one wants to belong to something, one wants to belong to a group, because belonging to a group is safe. One wants to be a tribal entity. And behind that there is fear, fear of being alone, of being left out—left out not only psychologically, but also one may not get a job. All that is involved in it and then you ask whether the mind can be free of conditioning. When you see the danger of conditioning, as you see the danger of a precipice or of a wild animal, then it drops away from you without any effort. But we don't see the danger of being conditioned. We don't see the danger of nationalism, how it separates man from man. If you saw the danger of it intensely, vitally, then you would drop it instantly.

So the question then is: Is it possible to be so intensely aware of conditioning that you see the truth of it?—not whether you like or dislike it, but the fact that you are conditioned and therefore have a mind incapable of freedom. Because only the free mind knows what love is.

Questioner: Is it true that the past should be consumed by the fire of present total involvement?

KRISHNAMURTI: What is the present? Do you know what it is? You say: "Live in the present," as many intellectuals advocate—they advocate it because to them the future is bleak (*laughter*), meaningless; therefore they say, "Live in the present, make the best of the present, be completely 'with it.'" We must find out what the present is. What is "the now"? Do you know what "the now" is, what the present is? Is there such a thing as the present? No, please, don't speculate about it, observe it. Have you ever noticed what "the now" is? Can you be aware of "the now," know what it is? Or do you only know the past, the past which operates in the present, which creates the future? Are you following? When you say "live in the present" you must find out what that present actually is. Is there such a thing? To understand if there is such a thing as the actual present, you must understand the past. And when you observe what you are as a human being, you see you are completely the result of the past. There is nothing new in you, you are secondhand. You are the past looking at the present, translating the present. The present being the challenge, the pain, the anxiety, a dozen things which are the result of the past, and you are looking at it getting very frightened and thinking about tomorrow, which again creates another pleasure—you are all that. To understand "the now" is an immense problem of meditation—that *is* meditation. To understand the past totally, see where its importance lies, and to see its total unimportance, to realize the nature of time—all that is part of meditation. Perhaps we can go into it another evening. But Sirs, before you can meditate there must be the foundation of righteousness, which means no fear. If there is any kind of fear, secret or obvious, then meditation is the most dangerous thing, because it offers a marvelous escape. To know what the meditative mind is, is one of the greatest things.

3

As we were saying yesterday, we are not concerned with theories, with doctrines, or speculative philosophy. We are concerned with facts, with what actually is. And in understanding "what is," nonsentimentally, nonemotionally, we can go beyond, transcend it. What is important in all these talks is not the idea, or the negation of the idea, but rather to be involved in the complexities of life, in the sorrow, with hopelessness and the lack of passion. The root of the word passion means "sorrow." We are using that word not with the implication of sorrow, or of the energy that comes through anger, through hate, through resistance, but rather in the sense of passion that comes naturally without effort when there is love. This evening we would like to talk about death, life and love.

We are not merely concerned with the description, with the explanation, but rather with the deep understanding of the problem, so that we are totally involved in it, so that it is the very breath of our life, not mere intellectualization. Can we look, understand and see what this whole problem of living is? Can we really come to grips with life, love and death—not analytically, not theoretically? To speculate about what lies beyond seems to me to be so vain, it has no value whatsoever. To understand the whole significance of life one has to examine what living is. Clever people thoughout the world have sought a significance beyond the living. The religious people have said this life is only a means to an end; and those who are not religious say that life is meaningless. Then they proceed to invent some significance according to their intellect, their conditioning.

We are not going to do that this evening. We are going to look at living as it is—not emotionally, nor sentimentally—but see actually what it is. And I think it is meaningful when one can look at the whole totality of living, not just at one fragment of it. Then perhaps, by not giving a meaning or a significance to life, we will see the beauty of living, the very vastness of it. And that beauty, the extraordinary quality of living, can only be understood, or felt deeply, if we examine profoundly what we call living, what we are actually doing. Without understanding what living is, we shall not be able to understand what dying is, nor what love is.

One uses the words "love," "death," and "living" so loosely—every politician talks about "love" and every priest has that word on his lips. Love and death, both are of immense importance, and I say that without understanding what death is, there is no understanding of love. To understand what death is, one has to understand most profoundly, with great earnestness, what living is; one must examine freely, actually without any hope. It doesn't mean we must be in a state of despair to examine. A mind that is in despair becomes cynical; nor can a mind that is burdened with hope examine properly, it is already biased. So to examine what we call living, the daily act of living, needs clarity, not of thought, but clarity of perception: the clarity of seeing actually "what is."

The seeing of "what is," that very act is passion! For most of us passion is always derived from hatred, from sorrow, anger, tension; or there is passion that is brought about through pleasure which becomes lust. Such passion is incapable of the energy that is required to understand this whole process of living. Understanding really *is* passion; without passion you can't do anything. Intellectual passion is not passion at all. But to examine the whole of living needs not only extraordinary clarity of perception, but also the intensity of passion.

So what is it that we call living? Not what we would like it to be—that's just an idea, it has no reality, it's merely the opposite of "what is." The opposite of "what is" creates division and in that division there is conflict. In looking at what living is, we should utterly banish the idea of what "should be," for that is escaping into ideological seeing, which is totally unreal. We are only going to examine what living actually is; and the quality of examination is more important than the examination itself. Any clever person can examine, given a certain sharpness of mind, a certain sensitivity. But if the exploration is merely intellectual it loses that sensitivity which comes when there is a certain quality of compassion, affection, care. To have that quality of mind that looks very clearly, there must be this care, this quality of affection and compassion, which the intellect will deny. We must be alert to the prompting of the intellect in the examination of what is actually going on in our daily life—one needs some warning, if I may use that word, to know that the description is never the described, nor the word the thing.

As we said, without understanding what living is, we shall never understand what dying is, and without understanding what death is, love merely becomes pleasure and therefore pain. What is it that we call living? As one observes in daily life, in every relationship with people, with ideas, with property, with things, there is great conflict. To us, all relationship has become a battlefield, a struggle. From the moment we are born till we die, living is a process of accumulating problems, never resolving them, of being burdened with all kinds of issues. Basically it is a field in which man is against man. So living is conflict. Nobody can deny that, we are all in conflict, whether we like it or not. We want to get away from this everlasting conflict, so we invent all kinds of escapes—from football to the image of God. Each of us knows not only the burden of that conflict, but also the sorrow, the loneliness, the despair, the anxiety, the ambition and the frustration, the utter boredom, the routine. There are occasional flashes of joy to which the mind immediately clings as something extraordinary and wants repeated; then that joy becomes a memory, ashes. That is what we call living. If we look at our own life—not verbally or intellectually, but actually as it is—we see how empty it is. Think of spending forty, fifty years going to the office every day, to accumulate money to sustain a family and all the rest of it. That's what we call living—with disease, old age and death. And we try to escape from this misery through religion, through drink, through erudition, through sex, through every form of entertainment, religious or otherwise. That is our life despite our theories, ideals and philosophy; we live in conflict and sorrow.

Our life has brought about a culture, a society, which has become the trap in which we are caught. The trap is built by us; for that trap each one of us is responsible. Though we may revolt against the established order, that order is what we have made, what we have built. And merely to revolt against it has very little meaning, because you will create another established order, another bureaucracy. All this, with the national, racial, religious differences, the wars and the shedding of blood and tears, is what we call living, and we don't know what to do. We are confronted with this. Not knowing what to do, we try to escape, or we try to find somebody who will tell us what to do, some authority, guru, teacher, someone who will say, "Look, this is the way."

The teachers, the gurus, the mahatmas, the philosophers, have all led us astray, because actually we have not solved our problems, our lives are not different. We are the same miserable, unhappy, sorrow-laden people. So the first thing is never to follow another, including the speaker. Never try to find out from another how to behave, how to live. Because what another tells you is not your life. If you rely or depend on another you will be misled. But if you deny the authority of the guru, the philosopher, the theoretician—whether communist or theological—then you can look at yourself, then you can find the answer. But as long as one relies and depends on another, however wise he may be, one is lost. The man who says he knows, does not know. So the first thing is never to follow another and that is very difficult because we don't know what to do; we have been so conditioned to believe, to follow.

In examining this thing called "living," can we actually —not theoretically—put aside every form of psychological following, every urge to find somebody who will tell us what to do? How can a confused mind find somebody who will tell the truth? The confused mind will choose somebody according to its own confusion. So don't rely or depend on another. If we do, we carry a heavy burden, the burden of dependence on books, on all the theories of the world; that is a tremendous burden and if you can put it aside then you are free to observe, then you have no opinion, no ideology, no conclusion, but can actually see "what is." Then you can look, then you can say: "What is this conflict that one lives with?"

As one observes—and I hope you are also observing, not depending on the words of the speaker—you will see this conflict exists as long as there is contradiction in oneself, the contradiction of opposing desires; as long as there is the opposite, the "what is" and the "what should be." The "what should be" is the opposite of "what is" and "what should be" is shaped by "what is." So the opposite is also "what is." Living is a process of conflict in which there is violence; that is "what is," the fact. The opposite is "nonviolence," a state in which there is no conflict, no violence. The man who is violent is trying to become nonviolent. It may take him ten years, or it may take him all the rest of his life to become nonviolent, but in the meantime he is sowing the seeds of violence. So there is the fact of violence and the nonfact, which is nonviolence, which is the opposite. In this contradiction there is conflict: the man trying to become something. When you can banish the opposite, not try to become nonviolent, then you can actually face violence. Then you have energy which is not dissipated through conflict with the opposite. Then you have the energy, the passion, to find out "what is."

Am I making this clear? You know, communication is quite arduous, but what is much more important than communication is communion: to commune together over this problem; that is, both of us at the same time, at the same level being intent to observe, to learn, to find out. Only then is there communion between two people, which goes beyond communication. We are trying to do both; we are not only establishing communication, but also at the same time we are trying to commune together over this problem. This is not propaganda, we are not trying to dominate you, or persuade you, or influence you, but merely ask you to observe.

Now I see that to observe, to see actually "what is," is not possible when there is the opposite. The ideal is the cause of the contradiction and therefore of the conflict. When you are angry and you say "I should not be angry," the "should not" brings about a contradiction and therefore there is a division between anger and the pretence that one should not be angry. To admit your anger and to be aware, to see the significance of that anger, you need energy and that energy is dissipated through conflict and through the pursuit of the opposite. So can you leave the opposite altogether? This is very difficult, because the opposite is not only the ideal but also it is the process of measuring and comparing. When there is no comparison then there is no opposite.

You know, we are trained and conditioned to compare, to measure ourselves against the hero, the saint, the big man. To observe "what is," the mind must be free of all comparison, of the ideal, of the opposite. Then you will see that what actually "is," is far more important than what "should be." Then you have the energy, the vitality, to put aside the contradiction which is brought about by the opposite. To be free of the process of comparison requires discipline and that discipline comes in the very act of understanding the futility of the opposite. To observe this closely, to see the whole structure and nature of this conflict, this very act of looking demands discipline; it *is* discipline. Discipline means learning and we *are learning*—not suppressing, not trying to become something, not trying to imitate, to conform. This discipline is extraordinarily pliable, sensitive.

Each one of us is examining this conflict. We said it arises through the opposite. The opposite is part of "what is." The opposite is also "what is." And as the mind cannot understand or resolve "what is," it escapes into "what should be." When you have put aside all that, then the mind is observing closely "what is," which is violence (we are taking that as an example). So what is this thing we call violence? When there is no opposite to violence, when you are actually faced with that fact of anger, the feeling of hatred—then is there violence, is there anger? Go into it, if I may suggest, you will see it in yourself. I can't go into it in too much detail because we have got to understand what death is, what love is; so we must proceed rather rapidly.

What we call living is conflict and we see what that conflict is. When we understand that conflict, "what is" is the truth and it is the observation of the truth that frees the mind from "what is." There is also much sorrow in our life and we do not know how to end it. The ending of sorrow is the beginning of wisdom. Without knowing what sorrow is and understanding its nature and structure, we shall not know what love is, because for us love is sorrow, pain, pleasure, jealousy. When a husband says to his wife that he loves her and at the same time is ambitious, has that love any meaning? Can an ambitious man love? Can a competitive man love? And yet we talk about love, about tenderness, about ending war, when we are competitive, ambitious, seeking our own personal position, advancement and so on. All this brings sorrow. Can sorrow end? It can only come to an end when you understand yourself, which is actually "what is." Then you understand why you have sorrow, whether that sorrow is self-pity, or the fear of being alone, or the emptiness of your own life, or the sorrow that comes about when you depend on another. And all this is part of our living. When we understand all this we come to a much greater problem, which is death. Please bear in mind that we are not talking about reincarnation, about what happens after death. We are not talking about that, or giving hope to those people who are afraid of death.

Yesterday we went into the question of fear. When the mind is free of fear, then what is death? There is old age with all its troubles: disease, loss of memory, a thousand ailments, the fear of aging. In this country all the old people are called young! A woman of about eighty is called a young lady! People are frightened and when there is fear there is no understanding; when there is self-pity there is no end to sorrow. So what is it to die? The organism comes to an end, obviously. Man lives for ninety years, and if the scientists discover some medicine he might live one hundred and fifty—and God knows why he wants to live to one hundred and fifty, the way we live! But even then, even if you live for one hundred years, the organism wears out, because we live so utterly wrongly: in conflict, fear, tension, killing animals and human beings. What a mess we make of our lives! So old age becomes a terrible thing. Yet there is always death—for the young, for the middle-aged or for the old. What do we mean by dying, apart from physical death, which is inevitable? There is a deeper meaning to death than merely the physical organism coming to an end; that is, psychologically coming to an end—the "me," the "you," coming abruptly to an end. The "me," the "you," that has accumulated knowledge, suffered, lived with memories pleasurable and aching, with all the travail of the known, with the psychological conflicts, the things that one has not understood, the things that one wanted to do and has not done. The psychological struggle, the memories, the pleasure, the pains—all that comes to an end. That is actually what one is afraid of, not what lies beyond death. One is never afraid of the unknown; one is afraid of the known coming to an end. The known being your house, your family, your wife, your children, your ideas, your furniture, your books, the things with which you have identified yourself. When that is gone you feel completely isolated, lonely, that is what you are afraid of. That is a form of death and that is the only death.

Seeing that—not theoretically, but actually—seeing that one is afraid of losing everything that one has owned or created or worked for, one asks: "Is it not possible to die psychologically every day, to everything that one has known?" Can one die every day, so that the mind is fresh, young and innocent each day? Actually do it and you will find out what extraordinary things happen. The mind then becomes innocent. An old mind, however experienced, is never innocent. Only a mind that has shed all its burdens every day, that has ended every problem every day, is an innocent mind. Then life has a different meaning altogether. Then one can find out what love is. Obviously love is not pleasure; as we said yesterday, pleasure brings pain because pleasure, like fear, is the process of thought. If love is the process of thought, then is it love? Most of us are jealous, envious, and yet we talk about love. Can an envious mind love? When one says one loves, is it love? Or is the mind protecting its own pleasure and therefore cultivating fear? Can love be cultivated when there is fear and pleasure, which is thought? And with it comes the problem of sex. (Laughter) Why do you laugh? I'm glad you laugh, but why?

We have to explore this question, as we have explored fear and what living is. Why have we made sex into such a big issue? Why has sex become such a problem? Apparently everything revolves around it, not only now, but also in the past. It has become such an extraordinarily important thing in life. Why? Would you please find out? We are not offering an opinion, we are examining. It has become so colossally important, first, because intellectually we are secondhand people. We know what others have done and do, we repeat what others have said—the Buddha, Christ, and all the others—we theorize. That is not intellectual freedom, which is freedom from thought. We are bound by thought, and thought is always old, it is never new; so intellectually there is no freedom in the deep sense of that word, because thought can never bring about that freedom. Intellectually we are bound and emotionally we are shoddy, ugly, sentimental, false, hypocritical. So in life we have lost all freedom, except in sex. That is probably the only free thing that you have. And with it goes pleasure, the image which thought has created about the act and we chew that image, that pleasure, like a cow chews the cud, over and over again. That is the only thing you have in which you are really free as a human being. Everywhere else you are not free, because we are slaves to propaganda whether it is Christian, Catholic, or Communist. Lacking freedom everywhere, there is only this freedom and that too is not freedom, because you are caught by pleasure and the responsibility of pleasure, which is the family. But if you really loved the family, the children, if you really loved with your heart, do you think you would have a single day of war?

Your security is in pleasure and therefore in that security there is pain, sorrow and confusion; and so in everything, including sex, there is pain, torture, doubt, jealousy, dependence. The one thing you have in which you feel free has also become a bondage. So seeing all this—actually, not verbally, not carried away by description, because the description is never the thing that is described—seeing it with your eyes, with your heart, with your mind, with complete attention, you will know what love is. And also you will know what death is, and what living is.

4

Man is searching for something more than the transient. Probably from time immemorial he has been asking himself if there is something sacred, something that is not worldly, that is not put together by thought, by the intellect. He has always asked if there is a reality, a timeless state not invented by the mind, not projected by thought, but a state of mind where time does actually not exist: if there is something "divine," "sacred," "holy" (if one can use those words), that is not perishable. Organized religions seem to have supplied the answer. They say there is a reality, there is a God, there is something which the mind cannot possibly measure. Then they begin to organize what they consider to be the real and man is led astray. You may remember the story about the devil who was walking down the street with a friend; they saw a man ahead stoop down and pick up something from the road. And as he picked it up and looked at it there was a great delight in his face; the friend of the devil asked what it was that he had picked up and the devil said, "It is truth." The friend said, "Isn't that a very bad business for you?" The devil answered, "Not at all, I am going to help him organize it." (*Laughter*)

The worship of an image made by the hand or by the mind and the dogmas and rituals of organized religion, with their sense of beauty, have become something very holy, very sacred. And so man, in his search for that which is beyond all measure, all time, has been caught, trapped, deceived, because he always hopes to find something which is not entirely of this world. After all, what actually have traditional, bureaucratic, capitalist, or communist societies to offer? Very little except food, clothes and shelter. Perhaps one may have more opportunities for work or can make more money, but ultimately, as one observes, these societies have very little to offer; and the mind, if it is at all intelligent and aware, rejects it. Physiologically one needs food, clothes and shelter, that is absolutely essential. But when that becomes of the greatest importance, then life loses its marvelous meaning. So this evening it might be worthwhile spending some time to find out for ourselves if there really is something sacred, something which is not put together by thought, by circumstances, which is not the result of propaganda. It would be worthwhile, if we could, to go into this

70

question, because unless one finds something that is not measurable by words, by thought, by any experience, life—that is, everyday living—becomes utterly superficial. Perhaps that is why (though maybe not) the present generation rejects this society and is looking for something beyond the everyday struggle, ugliness, brutality.

Can we inquire into the question, "What is a religious mind?" What is the state of the mind which can see what truth is? You may say "There is no such thing as truth, there is no such thing as God, God is dead, we must make the best of this world and get on with it. Why ask such questions when there is so much confusion, so much misery, starvation, ghettos, racial prejudices; let's be concerned with all that, let's bring about a humanitarian society." Even if this were done—and I hope it will be done—this question must still be asked. You may ask it at the end of ten, fifteen, fifty years, but this question will inevitably be asked. It must be asked whether there is a state which puts an end to time.

First of all there must be freedom to look, freedom to observe if there is such a state or not; we cannot possibly assume anything. So long as there is any assumption, any hope, any fear, then the mind is distorted, it cannot possibly see clearly. So freedom is absolutely necessary in order to find out. Even in a scientific laboratory you need freedom to observe; you may have an hypothesis, but if it interferes with the observation then you put it aside. It is only in freedom that you can discover something totally new. So if we are going to venture together, not only verbally but nonverbally, then there must be this freedom from any sense of personal demand, any sense of fear, hope or despair; we must have clear eyes, unspotted, unconditioned, so that we can observe out of freedom. That is the first thing.

In the past three talks we have found that there is the question of fear and pleasure. If that is not clear and if one has not applied oneself to the question of fear, then it will not be possible to follow further into what we are going to explore. Obviously our minds are conditioned by beliefs—

Christian, Hindu, Buddhist and so on. Unless there is complete freedom from belief of any kind, it is not possible to observe, to find out for oneself if there is a reality which cannot be corrupted by thought. And one must also be free from all social morality, because the morality of society is not moral. A mind that is not highly moral, a mind that is not embedded in righteousness, is not capable of being free. That's why it is important to understand oneself, to know oneself, to see the whole structure of oneself—the thoughts, the hopes, the fears, the anxieties, the ambitions, and the competitive, aggressive spirit. Unless one understands and deeply establishes righteous behavior, there is no freedom, because the mind gets confused by its own uncertainty, by its own doubts, demands, pressures.

So to inquire into this fundamental question as to what is the religious mind, and whether there is such a thing, there must be this freedom, not only at the conscious level, but also at the deeper levels of one's consciousness. Most of us have accepted that there is an unconscious, that it is something hidden, dark, unknown. Without understanding the totality of that unconscious, merely to scratch the surface by analytical examination has very little meaning, whether it is done by the professionals or through one's own inquiry. So one has to look into this also, into the conscious mind as well as into the mind that is deep down, secred, hidden, which has never been exposed to the light of intelligence, to the light of inquiry. Can we also go into the question whether the conscious mind—that is the everyday mind, the mind that has sharpened itself through competition, through so-called education—whether such a mind can examine the deeper, unconscious layers.

What is this treasured unconscious which everybody talks about? Must one go through all the volumes written by the specialists to find out? Must one go to an expert to tell us what it is? Or can one find out for oneself—completely, not partially, not in fragments? It is said that you must dream, otherwise you will go mad, because dreams are the hints, the intimations of the unconscious and the secret, unexplored layers of the mind. Dreams therefore are an expression of these deeper layers, and in this way, if you or the analyst are capable of interpreting the dreams, then you can expose, empty the unconscious. No one has ever asked why one should dream at all. It is said that you must dream, that it is healthy, normal; but one can question the validity of that statement because one must doubt everything. (This doubt gives you energy, vitality, passion to find out.) We must ask why one should have dreams at all, because if the mind is working all the time, is endlessly in movement night and day, then it has no rest, it cannot refresh itself, it cannot make itself anew. It is like a machine that is constantly working; it wears itself out. So one asks, as we are doing now, "What is the need for dreams?" It may be possible not to dream. After asking that question we are going to find out if it is possible not to dream, because the unconscious is the storehouse of the past, the racial and family inheritance, the tradition of society, the various formulas, sanctions and motives, the inheritance from the animal—it is all there. Through dreams these are revealed bit by bit and one must be capable of interpreting them rightly, That, of course, is quite impossible. There are experts who will translate all those dreams—but according to their conditioning, according to their knowledge, according to the information which they have derived from others.

So we are asking: is there a need for dreams? Is it possible not to dream? Consciousness is obviously not only of what is above, but also of what is below—the total thing. If during the waking day the content of the mind can be observed, watched, then when you sleep there will be no necessity for dreams. That is, if during the waking hours you are aware of your thoughts, of your feelings, of your reactions, your motives, the tradition, the inhibitions, the various forms of compulsion, the tensions—if you watch them, not correct them, not force them to be different, not translate them, but if you are actually choicelessly aware during the day—then the mind is so alert, so sensitive to every reaction, to every movement of thought, that the motives, the racial inheritance and all the rest of it are thrown up and exposed. Then you will see, if you do it seriously, with intensity, with a passion to find out, that your nights are peaceful, without a dream, so that the mind upon waking is fresh, clear, without distortion. The personal element is dissolved so that it can observe completely; this is possible, not by applying what the experts say, but through studying yourself as you watch yourself in the mirror when you shave, or when you comb your hair. Then you will find out that the whole of the unconscious is as petty, shallow, dull, as the superficial mind; there is nothing holy about the unconscious. Then the mind, being free from fear, from all the pain brought by pleasure, is not looking for pleasure. Bliss is not pleasure, bliss is something entirely different. Pleasure, as we pointed out, brings with it pain and therefore fear, but the mind is looking for pleasure —ultimate pleasure—because the pleasures that we have in this world are so worn out, they have become so dull and faded, and so one is always looking for new pleasures. But such a mind is always in a state of fear. A mind that is seeking everlasting pleasure, or wanting experiences that will assure great pleasure, such a mind is in darkness. You can observe this as a very simple fact.

So the mind, without being free from fear and the search for the deepening and the widening of pleasure—which brings pain and anxiety and all the burden and travail of pleasure—such a mind is not free. And a mind which believes that there is a God, or that there is no God, is equally a conditioned, prejudiced mind.

I hope you can do all that! The speaker is emphatic but don't be persuaded by him, for he has no authority at all. In this matter of finding out, there is no authority, there is no guru, there is no teacher. You are the teacher and the disciple yourself. If only one could put all authority aside, for that is the greatest difficulty—to be free and yet be established in righteousness, in virtue, because virtue is order. We live in great disorder; the society in which we live is in utter disorder, with social injustice, racial differences, economic, nationalistic divisions. As you observe in yourself, we are also in disorder, and the disordered mind cannot possibly be free. So order, which is virtue, is necessary; order, not according to some blueprint or according to the priests or those who say "We know and you don't know." Order is virtue and this order can only come about when we understand what is *disorder*. Through the negation of what is disorder, order comes into being. In denying the disorder of society there is order, because society encourages acquisitiveness, competition, envy, strife, brutality, violence. Look at the armies, the navies—that is disorder! When you deny—not society, but inwardly in yourself—fear, ambition, greed, envy, the search for pleasure and prestige—which breeds inward disorder—then in the total denial of that disorder there comes the order which is beauty, which is not merely the result of environmental pressures or environmental behavior. There must be order and you will find that order is virtue.

If one has done all this—and one must—then one can ask: "What is meditation?" It is only the meditative mind that can find out, not the curious mind, not the mind that is everlastingly searching. It is a peculiar thing, that when the mind is searching, it will find what it is searching for. But what it searches for and finds is already known, because what it finds must be recognizable—mustn't it? Recognition is part of this search, and experience and recognition come from the past. So in the experience which comes through search in which recognition is involved, there is nothing new, it has already been known. That's why people take drugs of various kinds; this has been done in India for thousands of years, it is an old trick to bring about the sharpening of the mind, to have new experiences; but one has never examined what experience itself means. One says one must have new experiences, new visions. When one has an experience, a new vision, say of Christ or of Buddha or of Krishna, that vision is the projection of your own conditioning. The Communist, if he has visions at all, will see the perfect state all beautifully arranged where everything is bureaucratically laid down. Or if you are a Catholic, you will have your visions of Christ or the Virgin and so on; it all depends on your conditioning. And when you recognize that vision, you recognize it because it has already been experienced, already known. So there is nothing really new in the recognition of a vision. A mind that is influenced by drugs, though it may temporarily become sharp and see something very clearly, what it sees is its own conditioning, its own pettiness, enlarged.

If you have done all this—and I hope you have done it for your own sake—we are now ready to enter into something that demands a great sense of perception, beauty and sensitivity. The word "meditation" has been brought to this country from the East. The Christians have their own words, contemplation and so on, but "meditation" has now become very popular. It is said by the yogis and gurus that meditation is a means to discover, to go beyond, to experience the transcendental. But have you asked who is the experiencer? Is the experiencer different from the thing he experiences? Obviously not, because the experiencer is the past with all its memories and when he experiences, transcends through meditation, or through taking a drug, he projects from the past, recognizes it and says, "This is a marvelous vision." It is nothing of the kind, because a mind burdened with the past cannot possibly see what is new.

We have now come to the point of finding out what meditation is. When you examine a method, a system, what is implied in it? Somebody says "Do these things, practice them day after day, for twelve, twenty, forty years and you will ultimately come to reality." That is, practice a method, whatever it is, but in practicing a method what happens? Whatever you do as a routine every day, at a certain hour, sitting cross-legged, or in a bed, or walking, if you repeat it day after day your mind becomes mechanical. So when you see the truth of that, you see that what is implied in all that is mechanical, traditional, repetitive, and that it means conflict, suppression, control. A mind made dull by a method cannot possibly be intelligent and free to observe.

They have brought Mantra Yoga from India. And you also have it in the Catholic world—*Ave Maria* repeated a hundred times. This is done on a rosary and obviously for the time being quietens the mind. A dull mind can be made very quiet by the repetition of words and it does have strange experiences, but those experiences are utterly meaningless. A shallow mind, a mind that is frightened, ambitious, greedy for truth or for the wealth of this world, such a mind however much it may repeat some so-called sacred word remains shallow. If you have understood yourself deeply, learned about yourself through choiceless awareness and have laid the foundation of righteousness, which is order, you are free and do not accept any so-called spiritual authority whatsoever (though obviously one must accept certain laws of society).

Then you can find out what meditation is. In meditation there is great beauty, it is an extraordinary thing if you know what meditation is—not "*how* to meditate." The "how" implies a method, therefore never ask "how"; there are people only too willing to offer a method. But meditation is the awareness of fear, of the implications and the structure and the nature of pleasure, the understanding of oneself, and therefore the laying of the foundation of order, which is virtue, in which there is that quality of discipline which is not suppression, nor control, nor imitation. Such a mind then is in a state of meditation.

To meditate implies seeing very clearly and it is not possible to see clearly, or be totally involved in what is seen, when there is a space between the observer and the thing observed. That is, when you see a flower, the beauty of a face, or the lovely sky of an evening, or a bird on the wing, there is space—not only physically but psychologically—between you and the flower, between you and the cloud which is full of light and glory; there is space—psychologically. When there is that space, there is conflict, and that space is made by thought, which is the observer. Have you ever looked at a flower without space? Have you ever observed something very beautiful without the space

77

between the observer and the thing observed, between you and the flower? We look at a flower through a screen of words, through the screen of thought, of like and dislike, wishing that flower were in our own garden, or saying "What a beautiful thing it is." In that observation, while you look, there is the division created by the word, by your feeling of liking, of pleasure, and so there is an inward division between you and the flower and there is no acute perception. But when there is no space, then you see the flower as you have never seen it before. When there is no thought, when there is no botanical information about that flower, when there is no like or dislike but only complete attention, then you will see that the space disappears and therefore you will be in complete relationship with that flower, with that bird on the wing, with the cloud, or with that face.

And when there is such a quality of mind, in which the space between the observer and the thing observed disappears and therefore the thing is seen very clearly, passionately and intensely, then there is the quality of love; and with that love there is beauty.

You know, when you love something greatly—not through the eyes of pleasure or pain—when you actually love, space disappears, both physically and psychologically. There is no me and you. When you come so far in this meditation, then you will find that quality of silence which is not the result of "thought seeking silence." They are two different things—aren't they? Thought can make itself quiet—I don't know if you have ever tried it. We struggle against thought because we see very well that unless it is quiet there is neither peace in the world nor inwardly—there is no bliss. So we try in various ways to quiet the mind through drugs, through tranquilizers, through the repetition of words. But the silence of the mind that is made quiet by thought is not comparable with the silence which freedom brings—freedom from all the things that we have talked about. In that silence, which is of quite a different quality than the silence brought about by thought, there is a different dimension. This is a different state which you have to find out for yourself; nobody can open the door for you, and no word, no description can measure that which is immeasurable. So unless one actually takes this long journey—which is not long at all, it is immediate—life has very little meaning. And when you do it you will find out for yourself what is sacred.

Do you want to ask any questions? Isn't this silence better than questions? If you are inwardly quiet, isn't that better than any question and answer? If you are really quiet, then you have love and beauty—the beauty that is not in the building, in the face, in the cloud, in the wood, but in your heart. That beauty cannot be described, it is beyond expression. And when you have that, no question need ever be asked.

FOUR TALKS AT STANFORD
UNIVERSITY

1

It is becoming more and more difficult to live peacefully in this world without withdrawing into a monastery or some self-enclosing ideology. The world is in such disorder, and there have been so many theories and speculative suggestions on how to live and what to do. Philosophers have been at it for so long, spinning out their ideas of what man is and what he should do. As one travels throughout the world—not being a philosopher or a human being crowded in with many ideologies and having no belief whatsoever about anything—one asks oneself whether it is at all possible for human beings to change.

When one asks that question (and I'm sure those of us who are somewhat thoughtful and serious do ask it), one hears it said that we should first change the world—that is, change the social structure with its economy—and that it must be a global change, a global revolution, not a change affecting only a part of the world. Then, it is said, there will be no need for the individual human being to set about changing at all: he will change naturally. Circumstances will then bring about right occupation, leisure, right relationship, consideration, love, understanding and so on. So there are those who, reasoning thus, advocate changing the environment—and it must be global—so that man, who is the creature of his environment, will also change, naturally.

We have this division, then, between the inner and the outer, the outer being the environment, the society. Bring about a deep revolution in the latter, they say, and this will result in changing the individual: the you and the me. This division has been maintained for thousands of years, the separation between what is called spirit, and that which is of the world, matter—the religious and the so-called worldly. And this division, in itself, is most destructive, because it breeds separateness and a series of conflicts: how the inner can adjust itself to the outer and the outer shape the inner. This has always been the problem. The whole Communist world denies the inner; they say, "do not bother about it, it will look after itself when everything is perfectly and bureaucratically organized."

One observes also that man, with all his anxieties, violence, despair, fear, acquisitiveness, his incessant competitiveness, has produced a certain structure which we call society, with its morality and its violence. So, as a human being, one is responsible for whatever is happening in the world: the wars, the confusion, the conflict that is going on both within and without. Each one of us is responsible, but I doubt whether most of us feel that at all. Intellectually, verbally, perhaps, we may accept it; but do we feel *actually* responsible for the war that is going on in Vietnam or in the Middle East, for the starvation in the East, and all the misery, division and conflict? I doubt it. If we did, our whole educational system would be different. As we do not feel it, we obviously do not love our children. If we did, there would be no war at all tomorrow; we would see to it that a different culture, a different education, was brought about.

So our question is whether a human being can be made to feel—not forcibly nor through sanctions and fear—that he must change *completely*. If he does not change, he will create a world (or, rather, perpetuate a world) in which there is misery, suffering, death and despair; and no amount of theory, theological speculation or bureaucratic sanctions are going to solve this problem. So what is one to do? Faced with all this confusion, strife, this antagonism, violence and brutality, what is a human being to do? How is he to act? I wonder if one asks this question seriously of oneself—not sentimentally, romantically, nor merely in an enthusiastic moment, but as a question constantly present in all its seriousness. And I wonder how we will answer? We might declare that it is not possible to change so deeply, immediately and fundamentally, as to create a new society. But the moment you say it is not possible, then it is settled: you have blocked yourself. If one says it is possible, then one is confronted with the question of how to bring about the psychological revolution in oneself. So, what is one to do? Escape by subscribing to some sectarian belief or by running away into a monastery where you practice Zen Buddhism? By joining a new cult or sect which promises everything you want?

Seeing the extraordinary division of the world into nationalites and religions, the Hindus, the Buddhists, the Christians, the Catholics and the divisions of races with all their prejudices; seeing that our minds are so heavily conditioned by the propaganda of the church, of the sacred books, of the philosophers and the theoreticians—facing all that—one asks oneself, "What am I, a single human being in relationship with the world, to do—what can I do?" When one puts that question to oneself, one must also ask, "What is action?" We ask "What am I to do and in relationship to what?" Must we deal with only a segment, a fragment of this total existence? Commit ourselves to only one part of this whole total existence, this whole life, and act according to that fragment as a specialist? Seeing this whole life—life of human sorrow, the human confusion, the utter lack of relationship, the self-isolating process of thought, the violence, the brutality of our life with all the fears, anxieties, tears, death and utter lack of compassion—seeing all this shall I and shall you deal with the *whole* of that, or with only a part of it? To deal with the whole of that, to be totally involved, we must be aware of ourselves as we are—not as we should like to be; aware of our minds, aware that we are violent, brutal, acquisitive human beings, and ask whether that can be transformed immediately.

The ideological state, which is nonviolence, freedom, love, doesn't exist: that's just an idea. What exists is what is. Can "what is" be transformed?—but not by becoming "what should be." We are conditioned to pursue the "what should be," the ideal, and it seems to me such a waste of time to pursue the ideal, the perfect, the extraordinary state that one imagines. When you pursue the ideal, the "what should be," it is a waste of energy, an escape from "what is." So, can the mind, which has been so heavily conditioned to accept the ideal, discard it completely and face "what is"? Because when we discard that which is false, we have the energy of the truth of "what is." That is, man's nature, inherited from the animal, is aggressive, violent, angry, full of hate and jealousy, whereas the ideal is to be nonviolent. This ideal, in turn, is put away at a great distance. And, if we are at all serious, we spend our time and energy in trying to become nonviolent. One can observe in oneself how heavily conditioned one is. There is this conflict between "what is" and "what should be," as there is always conflict when there is any form of division or separateness. There is conflict in our relationships because each one is isolating himself in his activities.

So, how is a mind that has been so heavily conditioned and which is now faced with "what is"—which is violence, hatred, anger and all the rest of it—how is that mind to be transformed? That, really, is the basic question affecting every one of us, psychologically. And how is this sense of separateness to end so that we can have real relationship? For it is only when there is no division that there will be no conflict.

We see that in endeavoring to transform that which is, man has invented an outside agency. Knowing that he is violent, brutal, angry and jealous, and that it will take too long to become perfect, he does not know what to do. So he invents an outside agency full of authority: God, an ideal, a guru, a teacher and so on—someone who will tell him what to do so that he can live in great peace, without conflict. But, when one discards all authority—and one must, because authority implies fear—when one discards the guru, the teacher, the outside agency, one is left alone with oneself. And that is a most fearsome thing: to be alone with oneself—without becoming neurotic or having all kinds of emotional upsets. When one has discarded all authority—thus becoming a teacher and disciple to oneself and not to another—then where is one? When you have no ideals and have nobody to guide you—because all the people who have tried to guide have led man astray, leaving him still unhappy, still confused, anxious and frightened—when you have come that far, where are you? When one discards the guru, the teacher, the authority, the ideal—when you *actually* do not depend on somebody psychologically—then what is one to do? Is there anything one can do?

You know, to communicate verbally is fairly easy. When we use the same language and give definite meanings to words, then it is fairly easy to communicate. But what is more important, it seems to me, is to commune with one another about these problems. Over this problem of life and living, therefore, there must not only be verbal communication but also, at the same time, a communion with one another. Then understanding becomes comparatively easy.

There is this question of fear, which is surely one of the most complex and confusing issues in our life. However much one may explain the causes of fear, describe the structure of fear, we must know that the word is never the thing, the description never the thing described. And not to be caught by the word or by the description, but to actually come into contact with that which we call fear, or with that which we call violence, means really to have direct relationship with what is. So one has to go into this question of the relationship between the observer and the thing observed. Take fear: is the observer different from the thing he observes? When the observer *is* the observed, then relationship is direct and possesses an extraordinary vital quality which demands action. But when there is a division between the observer and the thing observed, then there is conflict. All our relationships with other human beings—whether intimate or not—are based on division and separateness. The husband has an image of the wife and the wife an image of the husband. These images have been put together over many years through pleasure and pain, through irritation and all the rest of it—you know, the relationship between a husband and wife. So the relationship between the husband and the wife is actually the relationship between the two images. Even sexually—except in the act—the image plays an important part.

So when one observes oneself, one sees that one is constantly building images in relationship and therefore creating division. Hence there is actually no relationship at all. Although one may say one loves the family or the wife, it is the image, and therefore there is no actual relationship. Relationship means not only physical contact but also a state in which there is no division psychologically. Now when one understands that—not verbally but *actually*—then what is the relationship between the observer who says, "I'm afraid," and the thing called fear itself? Are they two different things? This brings us to the question as to whether fear can be wiped away through analysis. Does all this interest you?

Audience: Yes.

KRISHNAMURTI: Because if it doesn't, I'll get up and go and you can go. To me this is dreadfully serious. I'm not a philosopher, not a lecturer, nor am I representing some ancient philosophy from India—God forbid! (*Laughter*)

Having traveled the world over very often and talked to many people, one is confronted not only with the misery of the world but also with the utter irresponsibility of human beings, and one naturally becomes very, very serious. This does not mean to be without humor, but one does become extraordinarily serious and intense. And one *has* to be very serious and intense to solve these problems in oneself, because in oneself is the world, in oneself is the whole of mankind—although superficially we have different manners, different costumes and customs.

So, when one is serious, one is faced with the problem of whether the mind can actually be free of fear forever, and whether fear can be got rid of through analysis—through analyzing oneself day after day, or going to the professional to be analyzed, perhaps for the next ten years, paying out large sums if you have the money. Or is there a different way, a different approach to this problem, so that fear can end without analysis? Because in analysis there is always the observer and the thing observed; that is, the analyzer and the thing analyzed. And the analyzer must be extraordinarily awake, unconditioned, without bias or distortion in order to analyze; if he is at all twisted in any way, then whatever he analyzes will also be biased, twisted. So that is one problem in analysis. The other is that it will take a great deal of time, gradually and slowly, bit by bit, to remove all the causes of fear—by then one will be dead. (*Laughter*) In the meantime one lives in darkness, miserable, neurotic, creating mischief in the world. And, even after you have discovered the cause (or causes) of fear, will it have any value? Can fear disappear when I know what I am afraid of? Is the intellectual search for the cause able to dissipate fear? All these problems are involved in analysis because, as we admit, there is this division between the analyzer and the thing analyzed. Therefore analysis is not the way—obviously not—because one has seen the why and why not, one has seen the falseness of it, that it takes time and one has no time. Psychologically speaking there is no tomorrow: we have invented it. And so, when you see the falseness of analysis, when you see the truth that the observer is actually the observed, then analysis comes to an end.

You are faced with this fact that you *are* fear—not an observer who is afraid of fear. You are the observer *and* the observed; the analyzer *and* the thing analyzed. You know, when you see a tree, when you have actually looked at a tree—not verbally but actually—then you see that between you and the tree there is not only physical space but also psychological space. That space is created by the image you have of the tree, as "the oak," or whatever it is. So there is a separation between the observer and the observed, which is the tree. Can this separateness or space disappear?—not that you become the tree, that would be too absurd and have no meaning—but when the space between the observer and the tree disappears, then you see the tree entirely differently. I do not know if you have ever tried it.

Questioner: What exactly do you mean by the space between you and the tree disappears?

KRISHNAMURTI: Just a minute, Sir, let me finish, and then you can ask me questions afterwards. I hope you will. Analysis implies this space, and therefore there is no direct contact or relationship between the analyzer and the analyzed. And it is only when there is *immediate* contact with the thing called fear, that there is totally different action. Look, Sir, when you observe another—your wife, friend, husband—is that observation based on your accumulated knowledge of the person concerned? If so, that knowledge makes for separateness, it divides: hence there is conflict and therefore no relationship. So, can you look at another—now of course you can look at the speaker because he is going away and has no direct relationship with you—but can you look without that space at your wife, your children, your neighbor or your politician? If you can do that, then you will see things entirely differently.

You know, I have been told by those who are fairly serious and who have taken certain drugs—not for amusement, excitement or visions, but who have taken them to see what actually takes place—they have told me that the space between those who have taken it and the vase of flowers on the table disappears, and that therefore, they see the flower, the color, most intensely, and that there is a quality in that intensity which never existed before. We are not advocating—at least I am not—that you should take drugs, but, as we were saying, as long as there is space in relationship—whether between the analyzer and the analyzed, the observer and the observed, or the experiencer and the thing experienced—there must be conflict and there must be pain.

So, when this thing is really understood—not as an idea, not as a verbal exchange but actually felt—you will see that violence, which was experienced before as between the observer and the thing observed, that feeling of anger and hatred, undergoes a tremendous change: it is not what it was, a constant conflict from childhood to death, an everlasting battlefield in relationship, whether in the office or in the family. Being in conflict without being able to resolve it, fear comes into being. Fear also exists where there is pleasure. We are ever in pursuit of pleasure: that is what we want, greater and greater pleasure. And when we pursue pleasure, inevitably there must be pain and fear.

So our question this afternoon is whether the human mind can transform itself, not in time but out of time. That is, whether there can be a great psychological revolution inwardly without the idea of time. Thought, after all, is time, isn't it? Thought, which is the response of memory, knowledge, experience, is from the past. One can observe this for oneself as an actuality, not as a theory. Thought thinks about that of which it is afraid, or about that which has given pleasure, and the thinking about the pleasure and the pain lies within the field of time. Obviously. One experiences pleasure when one sees the sunset, or through various other forms of excitement and enjoyment, and so on. Thought thinks about that which has given excitement, enjoyment. Please do watch this: you can see it for yourself, it is so simple. Thinking about it gives continuity to that which one has enjoyed. Yesterday there was that lovely sunset. Instead of finishing with that sunset, which was over yesterday, we continue thinking about it, and the very activity of thought in regard to that incident breeds time. That is, I am hoping I shall have that pleasure again tomorrow. So thought breeds both pleasure and pain. Then, from this, arises a much deeper question: whether thought can be quiet at all. For it is only then that there is actual transformation.

Now do you care to ask any questions?

Questioner: *You spoke about being responsible, but I may not be responsible for my thought. Any change I want to make must be made with thoughts and perhaps I'm not responsible for my thoughts. I cannot determine what I think.*

KRISHNAMURTI: Sir, what do we mean by that word "responsible"? And is that feeling of responsibility the product of thought?

Questioner: No, and at the same time, yes.

KRISHNAMURTI: Look, Sir, is love the result of thought?

Questioner: No.

KRISHNAMURTI: Ah, wait! Go slowly Sir. (*Laughter*) Then, if you say no, what place has thought when you love?

Questioner: This would presuppose my understanding love.

KRISHNAMURTI: Ah, wait, Sir!—that is why I asked if love was pleasure. If it is pleasure then it is a product of thought. Then pleasure can be cultivated indefinitely—which is what we are doing. But love cannot be cultivated. Therefore love is not the product of thought. And when there is love, what is responsibility? Please go slowly. When responsibility is based on thought and pleasure, then there is duty involved in it, and all the rest of it. But when love is not pleasure—and one has to go into this very, very carefully—then has love (if I may use that word), has love responsibility in the accepted sense of that word? I love my family, therefore I am responsible for my family. Is that love based on pleasure? If it is, then that word responsibility takes on quite a different meaning: then the family is mine, I possess it, I depend on it, I must look after it. Then I am jealous, for wherever there is dependency, there is fear and jealousy. So we use this word "love" when we say, "I love my family, I'm responsible for it"; but when you observe a little more closely, you find children being trained to kill, being educated in that peculiar way so that they are always able to earn a livelihood, get a job, as though that was the end of life. So is all that responsibility?

Questioner: We can't really have will, because what we will is determined by our conditioning.

KRISHNAMURTI: Sir, what is will? Please see that these questions need a great deal of explanation, and everybody is getting bored or has to go away. We had better stop.

Audience: They just have to leave—they are not bored. Family responsibilities!

KRISHNAMURTI: You are not responsible for the people leaving? (*Laughter*) Right! You see, Sirs, we have exercised will: I must, I must not; I should, I should not. You have exercised will to succeed, to achieve power, position, prestige. You have exercised will to dominate. Will has played a great part in our lives. And, as you say, that is the result of the society, the environment, the culture in which we live. But the culture in which we live is, in turn, made by human beings, and so we must ask whether will has any place at all? Because will implies conflict, struggle, the contradiction: "I am this and I must be that. And to become that, I must exercise will." We are asking if there is not a different way of acting altogether, without will?

Questioner: If you don't use will, must you not then exercise thought?

KRISHNAMURTI: Look, I'll show you something. When you see danger, is there the exercise of thought or will? There is immediate action. That action may be the result of past thought. When you see a precipice, a snake, a dangerous thing, you act instantly. That action may be the result of past conditioning. Right? You have been told that it is dangerous to approach a snake, and that has become memory, conditioning, and you act. Now when you see the danger of nationality—which breeds war, the nations with their separate governments, separate armies and all the rest of these terrible divisions which are going on in the world —when you see the actual danger of nationality—see it, that is, not intellectually or verbally but *actually* see the danger of it, the destructive nature of it—is there an action of will? Does perception—the seeing of something as false or as true—does that demand thought? Is goodness the result of thought—or beauty, or love? And can thought ever be new?—because love must be new, love cannot be something that goes on day after day between the family and in the family, as a sort of private possession. Thought, on the other hand, is always old. So, can we, without the exercise of will, see things so clearly that there is no confusion and that there is therefore complete action?

Questioner: Complete action may be aesthetically pleasing.

KRISHNAMURTI: I don't know what you mean by "complete action." Why do we say aesthetically beautiful, while at other times it may also be very dangerous? What do we mean by "complete action"? Sir, take a very simple thing: when there is *comparative* action—that is, comparing which course of action is better—then there is measurement and good comes to an end. Right? No? When there is comparison, the good comes to an end. And, to be good —note that we are not using that word in the bourgeois sense—to be good completely means giving complete attention; when your whole body—eyes, ears, heart, everything—is given to attention. Sir, when you love, there is no less or more. *That* is complete action.

Questioner: Can I change my ideas or thought when, for example, every day when I go to the office they expect me to be ambitious, greedy and fearful; they put pressure on me to be that way and they show me that indeed I am petty, greedy, ambitious and fearful. Can I change if I see that this is not what I wish to be?

KRISHNAMURTI: Can I, belonging to a structure that demands that I be afraid, aggressive, acquisitive, can I go to the office without being ambitious? If I am not ambitious, if I am not greedy, completely—that is, actually and completely nongreedy, not just verbally—then nothing is going to make me greedy, because I have seen the truth and the falseness of greed. When I have seen that clearly, cannot I go to the office and not be destroyed? It is only when I am partially greedy (*laughter*) that I am caught. That is why one has to be complete—that is, completely attentive, so that in that attention there is a goodness which is not comparative, not measurable. When the mind is not greedy, no structure is going to make it greedy.

Questioner: How do I maintain attention in a painful situation, when instinctively my wish is to block out that painful incident?

KRISHNAMURTI: First of all, I do not want to block out anything. Neither pleasure nor pain. I want to understand it, look at it, go into it. To block out something is to resist; and where there is resistance, there is fear. The brain, the mind, has been conditioned to resist. So, can the mind see the truth that any resistance is a form of fear? Which means I must give attention to what is called resistance, be completely attentive to resistance: which is to block out, escape, take a drink, take drugs; any form of escape or resistance—be completely alert to it.

Questioner: How long can you do that, Sir?

KRISHNAMURTI: It is not a question of duration, of time, of how long. Do you see?—you are still thinking in terms of how long.

Questioner: My conditioning.

KRISHNAMURTI: Well, watch it, Madame, please do watch it. You flatter me or insult me: pleasurable or painful. I want the pleasurable and discard or resist the painful. But if I am attentive, I will be aware when the insult or the flattery is offered; I will see the thing very clearly. Then it is finished, isn't it? Next time you flatter me or insult me, it will not affect me. It's not a question of maintaining attention. When you desire to maintain attention, then you are maintaining inattention. Right? Do please go into it a little bit. An attentive mind does not ask, "How long will I be attentive?" (*Laughter*). It is only the inattentive mind that has known what it is to be attentive, which says, "Can I be attentive all the time?" So, what one has to be attentive to is *inattention*. Right? To be aware of inattention, not how to maintain attention. Just to be aware that I am inattentive, that I say things that I don't mean, that I am dishonest; just to be attentive. Inattention breeds mischief, not attention. So, when the mind is aware of inattention, it is already attentive—you do not have to do any more.

Questioner: How can you tell when you have true perception of what you should do, when one line of action is going to hurt someone and yet will benefit others?

KRISHNAMURTI: When you see something clearly as being true—and clarity is always true—there is no other action but the action of clarity. Whether it hurts or doesn't hurt is irrelevant. Look, nationality is poison: it has bred, and will continue to breed, wars and hatred. Now to be non-nationalistic will hurt a whole group of people: the military, the politician, the priest, all the flag wavers of the world. And yet I know it is the most dreadful thing, I see it as poison. What am I to do? I myself will not touch it. In myself I have wiped out all nationality completely. But the military will say, "You are hurting us." When one sees what is false and what is true, and acts, then there is no question of hurting or pleasing anybody. If you see that organized religion is not religion, then what will you do? Go to church to please people? It might hurt my mother if I don't. Sir, what *is* important is not what hurts and what pleases, but to see what is true. And then that truth will operate, not you.

2

We were saying yesterday that all our life is a constant struggle. From the moment we are born until we die, our life is a battlefield. And one wonders, not in the abstract but actually, whether that strife can end and if one can live completely at peace not only inwardly but also outwardly. While in actual fact there is no such division as the inner and the outer—it is really a movement—this division is regarded as existing, not only as the world inside and outside the skin, but also as the division between me and you, we and they, the friend and the enemy, and so on. We draw a circle around ourselves: a circle around me and a circle around you. Having drawn the circle—whether it is the circle of me and you, or the family, or the nation, the formula of religious beliefs and dogmas, the circle of knowledge one weaves around oneself—these circles divide us and so there is this constant division which invariably brings about conflict. We never go beyond the circle, never look beyond it. We are afraid to leave our own little circle and discover the circle, the barrier, around another. And I think that therein begins the whole process, the structure and the nature of fear. One builds a barrier around oneself, enclosing a private world very carefully made up of formulas, concepts, words and convictions. Then, living within those walls, one is afraid to go outside. This division not only breeds various forms of neurotic behavior, but also a great deal of conflict. And, if we abandon one circle, one wall, we build another wall around ourselves. So there is this constant, enduring resistance built of concepts, and one wonders whether it is at all possible not to have any division at all—to end all division and thus bring an end to all conflict.

Our minds are conditioned by formulas: my experiences, my knowledge, my family, my country, like and dislike, hate, jealousy, envy, sorrow, the fear of this and the fear of that. That is the circle, the wall behind which I live. And I am not only afraid of what is within, but even more so of what is beyond the wall. One can observe this fact very simply in oneself without having to read a great many books, study philosophy and all the rest of it. It may very well be because one reads so much of what others have said that one knows nothing about oneself, what one actually is, and what is actually taking place in oneself. If we looked in ourselves, ignoring what we think we should be but seeing what we actually are, then, perhaps, we would discover for ourselves the existence of these formulas and concepts—which are really prejudices and bias—that divide man against man. And so, in all relationships between man and man, there is fear and conflict—not only the conflict of sexual rights, of territorial rights, but also the conflict between what has been, is and what should be.

When one observes this fact in oneself—not as an idea, not as something that you look in at from outside the window—but actually see in yourself, then one can find out whether it is at all possible to uncondition the mind of all formulas, of all beliefs, prejudices and fears and thereby, perhaps, live at peace. We see that man, both historically and in present times, has accepted war as a way of life. So how to end war—not any particular war but all wars—how to live utterly at peace without any conflict, becomes a question not only for the intellect, but one that must be answered *totally*, not fragmentarily or in specialized fields. Can man—you and I—live completely at peace —which doesn't mean living a dull life, or one that has no active, driving energy—can we find out if such a peace is possible? Surely it must be possible, otherwise our life has very little meaning. The intellectuals throughout the world try to find a significance or assign a meaning to life. All the religious say that existence is only a means to an end, which is God—God being the real significance. If you happen not to be a religious person, then you will substitute the State for God, or invent some other theory out of despair.

So our quest, really, is to find out if man can live at peace; *actually* live it, not theoretically, not as an idea, not as your formula according to which you are going to live peacefully. Such formulas again become walls—my formula and your formula, my concept and yours, with resulting division and everlasting battle. Can one live without a formula, without division, and therefore without conflict? I do not know if you have ever put that question to yourself in all seriousness: whether the mind can ever be free of these divisions of the me and the not me? The me, my family, my country, my God; or, if I have no God, the me, my family, the State; and if I have no State: me, my family, and an idea, an ideology.

Is it possible to free oneself from all this, not eventually, but overnight? If we entertain the eventual theory we are not living at all: "eventually" we will be free, or "eventually" we will live at peace. Surely that is not good enough: when a man is hungry, he wants to be fed immediately. What, then, is the act that will free the mind from all conditioning—the act, not a series of acts? Here we have this self-centered activity which creates these divisions: the self-centered activity around a principle, an ideology, a country, a belief, around the family, and so on. This self-centered activity is separative and therefore causes conflict. Now, can this movement of the formula—which is the "me" with its memories, which is the center around which the walls are built—can that "me," that separate entity with its self-centered activity, come to an end, not by a series of acts but by one act completely? You know, we try to break down the conflicts little by little, chopping the tree little by little and never getting at the root of it. So one asks if it is at all possible, *by one act*, to end this whole structure of division, the separateness, the self-centered activity —all breeding conflict, war and strife. Is it possible?

When one asks that question in all seriousness, does one wait for an answer from another? After having that question put to you, are you waiting for an answer from the speaker? It is not that the speaker is avoiding answering, but are you waiting to be answered? If you are at all serious—and as we said yesterday, one must be because it is only a serious person that knows life, who knows what it is to live—will you wait for an answer? If you await an answer from the speaker, then the answer will be so many ashes, so many words, so many ideas, another series of formulas which, in themselves, will then become another cause for division: the Krishnamurti formula or somebody else's formula. But, if we do not wait for an answer from anybody—the speaker included—then we can take the journey together. Then it is your responsibility as well as the speaker's. Then you are not merely listening to words, to ideas. Then we are both walking together, which I think very important as we get rid of this division between the speaker and yourselves; we are together, discovering, understanding, acting, living—not according to any formula. Then there is direct relationship between us in taking a journey, because we are both feeling our way into reality: the reality—not the words, the description, the explanation or the philosophies of the cunning mind.

So, presuming that one is sufficiently serious, what is our problem? How to live our daily life here—not in a monastery or in some romantic dream world, not in some emotional, dogmatic, drug-ridden world—but here and now, every day; how to live at great peace, with great intelligence, without any frustration or fear, to live so completely, so in a state of bliss—which, of course, implies meditation —that, really, is the basic problem. And also whether it is possible to understand this whole life, not in fragments, but completely: be completely involved in it and not committed to any part of it; to be involved with the total process of living without any conflict, misery, confusion or sorrow. That is the real question. For only then can one bring about a different world. That is the *real* revolution, the inward psychological revolution from which springs an immediate outward revolution. Let us, then, take the journey together—and I mean together, not you sitting there and I sitting on the platform—to look together at this whole field of life so that we understand it; not for someone else to understand it and then tell us how to understand it. Then only will we be both teacher and disciple.

We see that these divisions, these formulas of the "me" and the "not me," and the "we" and the "they," behind which we live, breed fear. And if one can be aware of this overall fear, this total fear, then one can understand a particular fear. Merely trying to understand a particular, silly little fear, however garnished, will have no meaning until you understand the entire question of fear. Fear destroys freedom. You may revolt, but it is not freedom. Fear perverts all thought. Fear in oneself destroys all relationship. Please, these are not just words: this is evident in one's whole life—fear from the beginning to the end. Fear of public opinion, fear of not being successful, fear of loneliness, fear of not being loved, the measuring of ourselves against the hero of what "should be" and thus breeding more fear. This fear, moreover, lies not only at the obvious level of the mind but it also runs deep down. And we ask whether this fear can come to an end—not gradually, not bit by bit, but *completely*.

What is this fear? Why is one afraid? Is it because of what lies beyond the circle, or within the circle, or is it because of the circle? You follow what we mean? We are not trying to find out the particular cause of this fear, because, as we said yesterday, the discovery of the cause, the analytical process of understanding the cause and the effect, does not necessarily end fear—one has played that game for so long. But when one sees this fear—as one sees this microphone, actually what it is—is it within the wall, on the other side of the wall, or does it exist because of the wall? Surely it exists because of the wall, because of the division and not because you are within the wall or that you are afraid to look beyond the wall. It exists factually as it is, as you observe it, because of the wall. Now, how does this wall come into being?

Here please remember that we are taking the journey together and that you are not waiting for an answer from the speaker. We are taking the journey together, holding hands, and there is no point in your suddenly separating, taking away your hand and saying, "You walk ahead of me and tell me all about it." In journeying together, our verbal communication becomes more than mere communication: it becomes a kind of communion where there is affection, compassion and understanding because it is concerned with our common human problem. It is not that it was my problem and that I've resolved it and that therefore you have to accept my verdict. It is *our* problem.

How, then, does this wall of resistance, division and separation come into being? In everything we do, in all our relationships however intimate they be, there is this division bringing confusion, misery and conflict. How has this barrier come into being? If one could really understand it —not verbally, not intellectually—but *actually* see it and feel it, then one would find that it comes to an end. Let us go into it. We asked how this wall has come into being. I wonder what you would say had you to answer that. Now each one of us has an opinion or will offer an opinion—my opinion being right and your opinion wrong. Dialectically we can examine it, but we are not concerned with dialectical examination and reaching a definite conclusion. Truth is not to be found in opinion or conclusion. Truth is something that is always new and therefore the mind cannot come to it with a conclusion, with an opinion, a judgment; it must be free. So when we ask this question as to how this wall of resistance has come into being, we are not asking for an opinion or for some clever, erudite person to tell us how—because there is no authority. We are watching it together, examining it together, feeling our way into it.

Surely the wall has come into being through the mechanism of thought. No? Please do not reject it: just observe it: thought. If there were no thinking about death, you would not be afraid of death. If you were not brought up to be a Christian, Catholic, Protestant, Hindu, Buddhist or God knows what else: if you were not conditioned by propaganda, by words, by thought, you would have no barrier. And one can see how thought, as the "me" and the "you," brings this about. So thought not only creates this wall with its self-centered activities, but it also creates your own activity within your wall. So it is thought, in bringing about division, that creates fear. Thought *is* fear, as thought *is* pleasure. I see something very beautiful: a beautiful face, a lovely sunset, an enjoyable event of yesterday; thought thinks about it: how nice it was. Please do observe this:

how lovely that experience, and thought, by the very act of thinking, gives to that experience the continuity of pleasure. So thought is not only responsible for fear but also for pleasure. That is fairly clear, obviously. Because you have enjoyed the meal this afternoon, you want it repeated; or you have had some sexual experience, and thought thinks about it, mulls over it, chews it over, creates the picture, the image, and wants it repeated. This is pleasure repeated, which you call love. And thought, having created this circle, the barrier, the resistance, the belief, is afraid lest it be broken down, letting in something from beyond the wall. So thought breeds both fear and pleasure. You cannot possibly have pleasure without fear; they both go together, because they are the children of thought. And thought is the barren child of a mind that is only concerned with pleasure and fear. Please do observe it. Again let me remind you that we are taking the journey together: you are examining yourself, watching yourself in the mirror of the words.

So fear, pain and pleasure are the result of thought. And yet thought must function logically, sanely, healthily and objectively where it is needed in the technological world —not in human relationship, because the moment thought enters human relationship there is fear; then, in that, there is pleasure and pain. I am not saying anything crazy: you can see this for yourself. Thought is the response of memory, experience and knowledge and so is always old and therefore never free. There is "freedom of thought," certainly: that is, to say what you want. But thought itself is never free and can never bring about freedom. Thought can perpetuate either fear or pleasure but not freedom. And where there is fear and pleasure, love ceases to be. Love is neither thought nor pleasure. But to us love is pleasure and therefore fear.

When one is aware of this whole business of life as it is —not as we would like it to be, not according to some philosopher or holy priest, but actually as it is—one asks whether thought can have its right place and yet not interfere at all in every relationship. This does not mean a division between the two states of thought and nonthought. You see, Sirs, one has to live in this world, earn a livelihood, unfortunately, and go to the office. If ever there should come about a decent government of one world, then perhaps we might have no need to work more than a day, thereafter leaving the computers to take over, allowing us some leisure. But as long as that doesn't happen, one has to earn a livelihood and earn it efficiently and fully. However, the moment that efficiency becomes ugly through, for example, greed, or through this terrible desire to succeed and become somebody, the barrier of the "me" and the "not me" springs into being, bringing about competition and conflict. Realizing all this, how are we to live decently, efficiently, without ruthlessness and yet in complete relationship, not only with nature but also with another human being, in which there is no shadow of the "me" and the "you"—the barrier created by thought?

When one actually sees this thing that we are talking about—not verbally but actually—the very seeing, the actual seeing, is the act that brings down the wall of separation. When you see the danger of anything, such as a precipice or a wild animal and so on, there is action. Such action may well be the result of conditioning, but it is not the act of fear: it is the act of intelligence.

Similarly, to see intelligently this whole structure, the nature of this division, the conflict, strife, misery, the self-centeredness—to actually see the danger of it means the ending of it. There is no "how." So, what is important is to take the journey into all this—not led by another, for there is no guide—but seeing the world as it is: the extraordinary confusion, the unending sorrow of man, seeing it *actually*. Then the seeing of the whole structure of it is the ending of it.

Perhaps, if you care to, we can talk the thing over by asking questions. Yes, Sir?

Questioner: What does it mean to "actually" see something?

KRISHNAMURTI: Do you see your wife or your husband actually, or do you see them through an image, through a veil of opinions and conclusions—and therefore not at all? If so, no relationship can exist, for relationship means contact, to be related to. If the husband is ambitious, greedy, envious, seeking success, worried, beaten down, living in his own circle, and the wife also living in hers, where is the relationship? And yet that is what we call relationship: my family opposed to the rest of the world. If I *see* that, see the actual image through which I look—not an invented image but the actual image as it is—that very act of seeing the truth dispels the image.

You know, it is one of the most difficult things to ask a question. But we must ask questions, we must doubt everything on this earth: doubt our conclusions, our ideas, the opinions, the judgments—doubt everything—and yet also know when not to doubt. As with a dog on a leash, you must let him go sometimes, because out of freedom alone one discovers the truth. But to ask a question, the right question, needs a great deal of alertness, intelligence and awareness of the problem. I can ask casually without really entering into the problem, casually seeking an answer, but if I enter into the problem with my whole heart and mind, not trying to escape from it, in the very looking into that problem lies the answer. And therefore, when one asks a question—which doesn't mean that the speaker is preventing you from asking a question—when one asks a question one must be responsible not only for the asking but also for the receiving of the answer. How you receive the answer is much more important than how you ask the question, because the answer may be such that you do not like it at all. You may reject it because it does not, for the time being, please you, or because you do not see the value of it, or that you are thinking in terms of profit.

Questioner: I am not sure of the difference between thought, feeling, sensation and emotion.

KRISHNAMURTI: Sir, what is sensation? A stimulus. You see

103

a beautiful face, a lovely color. This perception is followed by sensation, then contact, then desire, with thought finally coming in and saying, "Ah! I wish I could have that!" There we have this whole movement of perception, sensation, contact, desire—which is strengthened by thought: "I want it," or "I do not want it"; "it is mine" and "it is not mine." The question then arises as to whether there can be perception of a beautiful face or a lovely sunset, without the interference of thought, or, in other words, can there be a state of nonexperience, but only perception—which is greater than all experiences. Have I explained it or am I saying something which sounds not very plausible and rather crazy? Look, Sir, there is the perception of a beautiful car (*laughs, joined by the audience*)—perhaps a beautiful face may be better (*laughter*)—then there is sensation: you want to touch it, look at it. Finally thought comes in and the whole machinery of pleasure and pain begins. Now, can there be observation of that face without the interference of the pain and pleasure principle? You understand what I'm talking about? Sir, this really is a very interesting problem.

We depend so much on others, psychologically. That dependence is based on fear and pleasure. Knowing the pain of dependence, one tries to cultivate freedom from dependence, but that very cultivation breeds other forms of fear, pain and conflict. One never asks why one depends, psychologically, on another. You depend on the milkman, the postman, and so on, but that is quite a different matter. But why this dependence psychologically, inwardly? Is it because one is lonely, that one has nothing in oneself, is insufficient to oneself? The very thing on which you depend is, is it not, the product of sensation and pleasure; therefore dependence is both the product and the cause of thought. Right? Which goes to show that experience is a complicated matter. And yet all of us are seeking greater and more meaningful experiences. We have never stopped to question the need, psychologically, of an experience. We have accepted, as we accept so many things, that experience is necessary for enlightenment, for understanding, for bliss, whereas, on the contrary, it is only a mind that is innocent that is capable of bliss—not a mind burdened with experiences. Moreover these experiences are based on this division of fear and pleasure, with every experience being discarded except those we like or dislike.

Questioner: Does true love require growth?

KRISHNAMURTI: Is there a false love? (*Laughter*) Sirs, do not laugh—it is so easy to laugh about things that touch one deeply. By laughter we put it away. Do we know what love is? Or do we know only the pain, the pleasure, the jealousy, the travail of that which we call love? Can an ambitious man, a competitive man, can a man who has specialized, know what love is? Can the man who is afraid of being a failure, or is struggling to become a success, know what love is? Can you ever have love and jealousy at the same time? Can a man or a woman who loves ever be jealous, ever dominate, possess, hold, be dependent? Actually all that we know is the pleasure and the pain of what we call love, which is generally translated into sex. So sex becomes an extraordinary problem. Not that we are against it—it would be terrible to be against anything—but one sees it for what it is. You know only the pain and the pleasure of what we call love, and therefore it is not love. Love cannot be cultivated—if it could, it would be marvelous; to cultivate it like a plant, water it, nourish it, look after it. If you could do that with love it would be very simple, but unfortunately it does not work that way. To love is quite a different thing in which there is no pain or pleasure. Therefore one must understand this fear and pleasure and all the rest of it, so that there is no division.

Questioner: The fact is that the world is in disorder and man in despair. That is the fact. What then can change man? Is it even possible?

KRISHNAMURTI: Sir, is the world separate from us? Are we not, each one of us, in disorder, confused—not merely superficially but in conflict: the conflicts of the opposites, the contradictions, the opposing desires? All that is disorder. And you ask whether it is worth changing all that. Is that the question?

Questioner: No, not exactly. There is this desire to change, but, confronted with the fact of the disorder in the world, what can be the nature of the change?

KRISHNAMURTI: The nature of the change is the negation of disorder. Disorder cannot be made into order. But the denial of disorder is the nature of the change: the very denial *is* the change. The negation of disorder is the positive nature of change. That is, I see disorder in myself: anger, jealousy, brutality, violence, suspicion, guilt—you know what human beings are. I'm aware of it. The mind is totally aware of all this disorder. Can it completely negate it, put it away? When it does so, through negation, the nature of change is the positive order. The positive can only come through the negative. Look, Sir, I see nationalism, the division of religions, the separateness that belief brings about, all the conflict, the disorder: I see that actually, feel it in my blood. And I put it away, not verbally, but *actually*: in myself I belong to no country, to no religion, subscribe to no dogma, no belief. Then that negation of what is false, which is the nature of the change, is truth.

Questioner: Doesn't this contradict what you said, that when you find jealousy within you, that you don't deny it, but that you become that jealousy?

KRISHNAMURTI: No, Madam. I said the observer *is* the observed. When there is the separateness on the part of the observer who says, "I am different from jealousy," then there is conflict between the observer and the thing observed. Let us go slowly. Like everything else, the human problem is really quite complex. So let us play with it a little bit and see it for ourselves. You know, when the wife is not me but is separate from me, there is no relationship. Then the "me" observes the wife as a separate entity, which division leads to conflict. That is clear. When the "me" is separate from its jealousy, there is conflict; such as: "how to get rid of it, it is right to be jealous, it is enjoyable to be jealous, it is part of love to be jealous," and all the rest of it. But when there is no division between the observer and the thing he calls jealousy, he *is* that. He does not become jealousy, he *is* it. Then what will you do? You understand the problem?

Audience: That is what the lady is asking, Sir. She asks how can you negate that which you are. You said to negate disorder is change and the lady asks: "If I am the disorder, how can I negate it?"

KRISHNAMURTI: Ah! I will explain. How can I negate disorder if I am disorder? I am the nation, I am the belief, the disorder. If the "I" negates disorder, that very I, which is separate, will create yet another form of disorder. That is your question, Madam? Right. When you say "negate disorder," what do you mean by that? Who is there to negate disorder? Please follow this slowly, step by step. This disorder is the cause of thought: my belief and your belief, my God and your God, my formula and your formula, my prejudice opposed to your prejudice. So I am that disorder and thought is that disorder, because I am thought. Right? Thought is me and the "me" is disorder. So, when one negates this, one negates thought, not disorder: not "I" negate it. Look, I am disorder. This disorder is created by thought, which is me and which brings about separation. That's a fact. What, then, is the negation of this fact? Who is it that is going to deny this disorder and put it aside? What is it that is going to change this? Is that clear? Now the negation of disorder is silence. Any movement of thought will only breed further disorder. Then you will ask, how thought is to come to an end, who is to bring to a stop this perpetual motion that is going on night and day?

Thought itself must deny itself. Thought itself sees what it is doing—right?—and therefore thought itself realizes it has to come of itself to an end. There is no other factor than itself. Therefore when thought realizes that whatever it does, any movement that it makes, is disorder (we are taking that as an example), then there is silence. The nature of the change from disorder is silence. I do not know if you've ever seen or felt the quality of silence: when the mind and the body are extraordinarily quiet. That is, when you want to see something very clearly, when you want to hear something that is being said with all your heart and mind, your body is quiet and your mind is quiet. It is not a trick. It is quiet. In the same way, disorder and the manner of change are resolved only when there is complete silence. It is silence that brings about order, not thought.

Questioner: Does man always try to possess that which is pleasurable to him?

KRISHNAMURTI: Don't we all do that? Don't we all want to possess that which has given us pleasure—a picture on the wall, a building, a woman, a man? So, when we possess a piece of furniture that we like, we *are* the furniture. And pain is involved in that possession as it might get lost. That is why we cling to our husband, our wife, the family. The marvelous circle is woven around the family, bringing it into battle with the rest of the world. One asks whether the family could exist without the circle, without the wall. Those of you who have a family should try it and see what happens. You will see something totally different taking place. Then perhaps you will know what love is and see with your own eyes the nature of the change that love brings about.

3

Of the many things we might talk over together, one of the most obvious and important is about why we do not change. We may change a little bit, here and there, in patches, but why do we not fundamentally change our whole way of behavior, our way of life, our daily nature? Technologically the world about us is advancing with extraordinary speed, while inwardly we remain more or less the same as we have been for centuries upon centuries. Caught as we are in this trap—and it is a dreadful trap—one wonders why we don't break through, why we remain heavy and stupid, empty, shallow minded, superficial and rather dull. Is it because we do not know ourselves? Leaving aside the ideas of the various specialists, with their peculiar assertions and dogmas, we see that we have never really investigated ourselves, gone into ourselves deeply to find out what we actually are. Is that the reason why we do not change? Or is it that one has not got the energy? Or because we are bored—not only with ourselves but also with the world, a world which has very little to offer except motor cars, bigger bathrooms and all the rest of it? So we are bored outwardly and, probably, also with ourselves because we are caught in the trap and don't know how to get out of it. It is also likely that we are very lazy. Furthermore, in knowing ourselves there is no profit, no reward at the end of it, whereas most of us are conditioned by the profit motive.

These, then, may be some of the reasons why we do not change. We know what the trap is, we know what life is, and yet we go trudging along monotonously and wearily until we die. That seems to be our lot. And yet, is it so difficult to go into ourselves very deeply and transform ourselves? I wonder if one has ever looked at oneself, known oneself? From ancient times this has been reiterated over and over again: "Know thyself." In India it was postulated, the ancient Greeks repeated the advice, while modern philosophers are also attempting to say it, complicated only by their jargon and their theories.

Can one know oneself—not only at the conscious level but also at the deeper, secret levels of the mind? Without self-knowledge, surely, one has no basis for any real, serious action, no foundation upon which to build clearly. If one doesn't know oneself, one lives such a superficial life. You may be very clever, you may know all the books in the world and be able to quote from them, but if you do not know yourself, how can you go beyond the superficial? Is it possible to know oneself so completely that, in the very observation of that total self, there is a release? Perhaps we can go into this question together this afternoon, and, in so doing, we may also come upon what love is and what death is.

As human beings, I think we should be able to find out

what death is while still living; and also what love is, because that is part of our life, our daily living. Can we inquire into ourselves without any fear or bias, without any formula or conclusion, to find out what we are? Such an inquiry demands freedom. One cannot inquire into oneself, or into the universe of which one is a part, unless there is freedom—freedom from hypotheses, theories and conclusions, freedom from bias. Moreover, to inquire one needs a sharp mind, a mind that has been made sensitive. But the mind is not sensitive if there is any form of bias, thus rendering it incapable of any real inquiry into this whole structure of the self. So let us go into this question together, not only through verbal communication but also nonverbally, which is much more exciting and which demands a much greater energy of attention. When one is free to inquire, one has the energy. One has not got the energy, the drive, the necessary intensity, when one has already reached a conclusion, a formula. So, for the time being, can we put away all our formulas, conclusions and biases about ourselves—what we are, what we should and should not be and all the rest of it—put these aside and actually observe?

One can only observe oneself in relationship. We have no other means of seeing ourselves because (except for those who are completely neurotic) we are not isolated human beings: on the contrary, we are related to everything about us. And in that relationship, through observing one's reactions, thoughts and motives, one can see, nonverbally, what we are.

Now what is the instrument of observation, what is the thing that observes? About this we must also be very clear. Is it an observation from outside the window looking in, as in at a shop window, or are you watching yourself from within and not from without? If you watch yourself from the outside, then you are not related to "what is." I think one should be very clear about this. One can observe oneself looking over the wall, as it were, in which case such observation is rather superficial, unrelated, inconsequential and not responsible. When one analyzes oneself, there is always the analyzer and the thing analyzed. The analyzer is the one looking over the wall, judging, evaluating, controlling, suppressing and so on. But can one watch oneself intimately, actually as one is? That is, can one watch oneself without the thinker, the observer?—the observer who is always outside, who is the censor, the entity that evaluates, saying, "This is right," "This is wrong," "This should be," "This should not be"—all of which renders one's observation very limited and merely according to the social, environmental and cultural conditioning.

So we have this very real problem: how to observe—not as an outside observer who has already come to certain conclusions about himself—but merely to observe. To be choicelessly aware, without a directive, without deciding what one should or should not do, but merely to observe what is *actually* going on. To do that there must be freedom from every form of conclusion and commitment. So, to observe nonverbally, to observe without the barrier of an outsider who is looking in, there must be freedom from all fear and all sense of correction. If one has such an instrument, then one can proceed to find out. But, because one has already banished all the things that make for a center from which an observer looks at the observed, what is there to find out?

One wants to look at oneself with clear eyes, with unspotted eyes, without the interference of the conventional, respectable social morality—which is no morality at all. When one has put aside the conclusion and the formula, fear, any desire to be other than what one is, then what is there? What we are is a series of conclusions. What we are is actually a series of experiences based on pleasure and pain, memories, the past. We *are* the past; there is nothing new in us. When one thus observes oneself freely—and to be free, one has to have set aside all these things—what is one actually? I wonder if you have ever put that question to yourself? What is one's relationship with this whole business of what is called living? And what is living, as it

111

is? One can, of course, readily see what it actually is: an everlasting struggle, a battlefield which we call living, conflict—not only with another but also within ourselves—pain, fleeting moments of great joy, fear, despair and a series of frustrations; the contradictions in ourselves both at the conscious and the deeper levels; a state of nonrelationship; great sorrow—which is generally self-pity—loneliness and boredom. Then the escape from all this into religious beliefs: your God and my God. That is our life as it actually is. Going to the office for forty years—you know, so proud about all this; aggressive, competitive, brutal. That is our life and we call that living. And we don't know how to change it. We are eager to change the superficial structure of society—a new bureaucracy instead of the old one, and so on. However, the outward change has meaning only when there is deep inward revolution: then the outer and the inner are the same movement, not two separate movements.

So, seeing all this, the insanity of it, why do we not change it? I wonder if one really does see this, our living as it actually is; or does one see it only verbally—and here one must realize that the description, the explanation, is never that which is described or explained. Knowing all this, seeing all this vast confusion, misery and travail, why do we accept it, why do we go on with it? Do we look to another to help us out of it? There have been teachers, gurus, saviors—oh, an innumerable number of these—but here we still are. So one loses, or has lost, all faith in another. And I hope you have. This doesn't mean that one becomes cynical, bitter and hard, but that one sees the actual fact that, inwardly, no one can help us. Recognizing all this, the actuality of life as we live it everyday, the torture and the aching misery of it, why doesn't one apply oneself completely and utterly to the understanding of it all and break through it? What is education for if we do not do this? What is the good of your becoming Ph.D.'s and all the rest of it, if all this is not fundamentally changed?

We must now ask what is the nature of the energy that is required to break out of this trap, this vicious circle in which one is caught. What provides the necessary drive? Obviously it cannot be verbal, nor can it stem from the assertions or conclusions of another. The nature of this energy is freedom—the demand to be free. By freedom we do not mean doing what you like, licentiousness, revolt, undisciplined activity and so on. Freedom is not lack of discipline: on the contrary, freedom demands great discipline. Please note here that while the word "discipline" is an ugly word for most people, it actually means to learn. That is the root meaning of the word: to *learn*, not to conform; not to imitate but to learn, not to obey but to find out. Learning or finding out, in itself, brings its own discipline. Therefore discipline, which is to learn, is a constant movement and not mere conformity to some pattern. When one understands that—not verbally but actually, sees the truth of it, feeling it in your very bones—then you will have the energy to break through this conditioning of fear, this anxiety, these aching sorrows.

In the understanding of this whole psychological structure of ourselves, there are these two vital questions: what is living—which we have tried to find out—and also what are love and death. For that is part of our living, and the sanctity of living lies in the discovery of what love is and what death is. Such sanctity comes only of living in the now—not having lived or living in the future—and in that we can perhaps discover what love is and what death is. Then again, without knowing what love and death are, we cannot know what living is.

What is death, of which most of us are so frightened? Can a living human being, sane, rational, healthy and not morbid, find out what dying means?—and here we do not mean when one is old and decrepit, diseased and on the point of slipping away unknowingly. Does this question have any interest at all? Not so much to the older generation, perhaps, as we have had most of our time, but it is a question that really applies to everybody—the young, the middle aged, the aged and the dying. Just as we tried to find out what living is—and which, not being this battlefield, this conflict, this misery, becomes therefore something extraordinarily sacred (if I may use that word without your attempting to belittle it)—in the same way, to find out what death is.

I wonder what your reaction is to this question. Either you are afraid, or you have theories, or you believe: believe in the life hereafter—reincarnation for example, which the whole of the East believes in. They believe in reincarnation, but they don't behave in this life; only it is a very comfortable theory in that you will have another chance. But, putting that aside altogether, to understand the now, one must understand the past. You cannot say, "I'm going to live in the now"—it has no meaning because the now is the passageway of the past to the future. When you say to yourself, "I'm going to live in the present," the "you" who is going to live is the result of the past. You may draw a circle around yourself, saying, "This is the now or the present," but the entity that is living in the now is the result of the past: he is entirely the past. To live now, in the present—not ideologically, not from a conclusion nor as an assertion—but actually to live completely in the present, means that one must be unconditioned and free.

Asking oneself what it means to die, what death is, is not a neurotic question: on the contrary, it shows that one is very healthy, sane and balanced, otherwise one wouldn't ask that question. It means that one is no longer frightened to find out. Obviously the body goes, the organism collapses through constant wear and tear. It can be made to last a little longer if one lives fairly sanely, without too much pressure, strain or excitement. Or the doctors and the scientists may invent a pill or something that will give you another forty or fifty years—although I do not see the point of living another fifty years in this trap. In asking what dying is, one must also ask what it means to actually live—if one can so live—without all the travail: that is, to end the way of living as we know it. Because that is what is going to happen when one dies: the end of everything. The soul, or the Atman as the Hindus call it, is just a word. One doesn't know if there is a soul, a permanent "something." Is there anything permanent in us, or do we only wish there were something permanent? When one observes oneself, there is nothing permanent: everything is in movement, in a state of flux. And when one dies, one dies to everything that one has known: the family, the children, the job, the books that one wanted to write or has written, the experiences, all the accumulations that one has piled up, and the responsibilities. There is the ending, psychologically as well as physically, of all that is known. That is death. I think most of us would agree to that.

Now, can one die every day to everything that one knows —except, of course, the technological knowledge, the direction where your home is, and so on; that is, to end, psychologically, every day, so that the mind remains fresh, young and innocent? That *is* death. And to come to that there must be no shadow of fear. To give up without any argument, without any resistance. That is dying. Have you ever tried it? To give up without a murmur, without restraint, without resistance, the thing that gives you most pleasure (the things that are painful, of course, one wants to give up in any case). Actually to let go. Try it. Then, if you do it, you will see that the mind becomes extraordinarily alert, alive and sensitive, free and unburdened. Old age then takes on quite a different meaning, not something to be dreaded.

One also has to find out for oneself what love is. That word is one of the most loaded of words; everybody uses it and its usage ranges from the most cunning to the most simple. But what is it actually? What is the state of the heart and the mind that loves? Is love pleasure? Please do ask these questions of yourself. Is love desire? If it is pleasure, then with it must go pain. If pleasure and pain are associated with love, then it is obviously not love. As you will recall, we saw that pleasure is the product of

115

thought. Thinking about the sexual experience that you had—chewing it over, the building of the image—is to sustain the pleasure of that experience. Thought engenders pleasure and it also breeds fear: fear of tomorrow, fear of the past, thinking about what one did, thinking about the physical pain that one has experienced and fearing a recurrence. So thought breeds pleasure, fear and pain and are these to be called love? But that is all we know. That is what we call love. I love my wife and when that wife, on whom I depend for sex, for cooking my meals and running the family, when she turns and looks at another, I am angry, furious and jealous—and this is called love. Then man invents the love of a God—a God who doesn't demand anything, who doesn't turn his back on you. You have him in your pocket and are sure he is there protecting you in your jealousies, in your anxieties, leading you on to even greater cruelty.

All this is called "love," but is it? Obviously not, because love is not something that is the product of thought. Love cannot be cultivated. Love cannot be bought through pleasure. How can an aggressive, ambitious, competitive man love? And if he wants to find out what it is—actually and not theoretically—he has to end his ambition, his greed, his hate of another, putting aside completely all that which is not love. But, you see, we play with all these things and then talk about love. We are really not very serious people, and because we are not serious, our life is what it is. So, without dying there is no love, for love is always new and not a routine matter of sex and pleasure. For most of us, throughout the world, sex has become an extraordinary problem, or, rather, a problem in which we delight. Do you never wonder why this is so? It would seem as though it has just been discovered for the first time, being featured in every magazine and all the rest of it. Why has it become such a persistent and continuing problem with which the word "love" is associated? Probably the clever ones will put up many arguments as to why man gets so excited about this one thing. But, leaving aside all the experts and the intellectual gurus, can one see why one is so caught up in this thing?

You will have to answer this question; you cannot just brush it aside, because it is a part of our life, part of this thing called life which has become such a battle and such a misery. Why has sex become a problem? Or should we rather ask why it is apparently the only thing left to man in which he is free? Therein he loses himself totally: at that moment he is no longer all the miseries, all the memories, the tortures, the competition, the aggression, the violence and the battling. He simply is not there. So, because he is absent, it has become important; then there is no longer the division between "me" and "you," "we" and "they." Such division comes to an end, and at that moment perhaps you find great freedom. Probably it has become so extraordinarily important just because it is the only thing we have left in which we can find such freedom. In everything else, we are not free. Intellectually, emotionally and physically, we are constrained and restricted secondhand people, thoroughly molded by our technological society. So, with no freedom except in sex, sex has become important and, because of that, a problem. We are not saying you should not have sex—that would be absurd. But can we cease to be slaves, secondhand human beings endlessly repeating what we have been told about things that actually do not matter very much, endlessly living in an ideological world—that is, living with formulas and therefore not actually living at all? Then, when one is free all around, both intellectually and in one's heart, perhaps this problem won't be serious.

Observing all this, from the beginning to the end and noting that we do not change at all, one must ask why one has not got the energy to change. We have the tremendous and extraordinary energy required to go to the moon but not enough, apparently, to change ourselves. And yet I assure you that it is one of the easiest things to do, and that it becomes easy when you know how to look. When you can *actually* see "what is," without trying to change it, suppress it, go beyond it or escape from it, then you will see that "what is" undergoes a tremendous change. That is, when the mind is completely silent in observation, then there is radical change. And the watching of all this, the observing of it deeply in oneself, brings us to one more question, which is: What is meditation?—because a mind which is not meditative cannot understand this whole structure and chain of our life. Perhaps we can discuss tomorrow the state of the mind which is religious, not belonging to some stupid organization but remaining free and therefore religious; that is, the state of the mind which is in the act of meditation. This is not an invitation for you to come tomorrow. (*Laughter*)

Perhaps, if you care to, we will now have some questions

Questioner: Why does each one of us have the "I" structure? What is its origin?

KRISHNAMURTI: The questioner asks why there is a separate "me." Why is there this peculiar entity that thinks it is so very different from the other entities? Why is there this "me" with all its problems, and the "you" with all your problems—which is also the "me"? The "me" is not different from the "you" because you have the same problems, only you clothe them in different words, using different ways of expressing them. But it is still the "me," expressing itself differently. I, born in India and educated abroad, and you here and educated here, with your problems; and if I have problems, what is the difference between you and me? —not physically, of course: you may have a bigger bank account, a bigger house and a nice car. You may have more abundance of things than the other, but, apart from a better superficial education and the chance of expressing it, a better job and all that, is there any basic difference? If there is no difference, why all this fuss about it—you and me, they and I, we and they, the black and the white, the yellow and the brown—why? There is great pleasure in being separate, all the vanity of it: I am original, unique, marvelous, and you say exactly the same thing, only putting it in a minor key. This vanity that each of us is so extraordinarily unique, gives great pleasure.

Are we unique? You have sorrow and so has the other; you are as confused as the other; uncertain, anxious, aggressive, brutal, suspicious, guilty as is the other. So when we free ourselves from this basic division of the "I" and "you," the "we" and "they," is there then any division at all? Is not the observer then the observed, which is you? In that there is vast compassion. It is only when I have built a wall around myself and you have built a wall around yourself, leading to resistance, that the whole misery begins. The social structure, too, encourages this "me" and this "you." Can we not be free of this division in our thoughts and in our society, which our own vanity has cultivated? Then, if you have gone that far, you will probably find out what love is.

Questioner: Would you say something about the effort that sometimes gets in the way when one tries to be aware?

KRISHNAMURTI: What is effort? Why should we make effort? I know it is the accepted tradition that you must make an effort, otherwise you will be a nobody, just a God knows what. So, at all costs, make an effort: that is the conditioning, the tradition, the accepted norm. Now, Sir, what is effort and why do we have to make an effort? This is a very important question. Is there any effort when there is no contradiction? Please follow this. When the "me" *is* "you" —which really requires a tremendous depth of feeling and understanding: you cannot just state that the "me" is "you," as it would have no meaning—when they are one in relationship and thus without contradiction, what need is there for effort? There is no effort. There is effort only when there is a psychological contradiction, that is: the "what is" over and against the "what should be," the opposite—which is the contradiction. The "what is" trying to become the "what should be," violence trying to become nonviolent—in this lies the contradiction and therefore the effort, the endeavor to become something which is not. So, basically, effort implies contradiction: I am this but I will be that; I am a failure but, by Jove, I'm going to become a success; I am angry but I will cease being angry, and so on. A series of corridors of opposites and, hence, conflict.

Speaking psychologically, is there an opposite? Or is there always only "what is"? Because the mind does not know how to deal with "what is," it invents the opposite, the "what should be." If it knew how to deal with "what is," there would be no conflict. If the mind could cease measuring itself against the hero, the perfect, the glorious and all that, it would be what it is. Then, free of all comparison, free of the opposite, the "what is" becomes something entirely different. In that there is no effort involved at all. Effort means distortion and effort is a part of will, which distorts. But to us will and effort are our bread and butter; we are brought up on it: you must be better than that boy in the examination—all that. And in being brought up like that lies great mischief and misery. So, to see "what is" and to be aware of that *without any choice*, frees the mind from the contradiction of the opposites.

Questioner: You said yesterday that if one could get rid of the circle around the family, that an extraordinary thing would happen. I would like very much to understand that.

KRISHNAMURTI: First of all, *is* one aware—not verbally—that there is a wall around oneself? Each one of us has a wall around himself: a wall of resistance, of fear and anxiety. The "me" built around myself, thus making the wall; this "me" in the family, each member of which is also surrounded by his own wall. Then the whole family with a wall around itself and similarly, with the community and the society. Now is one aware of this? Do we not feel that living in this world, it is necessary, otherwise the "me" will be destroyed and so will the family? So we maintain the wall as the most sacred thing. Now if one is aware of it, what happens? If one removes altogether this wall around oneself, around the family, does the family end? What then happens to the competition between the "me," the family, and the rest of the world? We know very well what takes place when there *is* a wall—then we have resistance, conflict, everlasting battle and pain, because any separative movement, any self-centered activity, does breed conflict and pain. When there is an awareness of the whole nature and structure of this circle, this wall, and an understanding of how it has come into being—that is, the immediate realization of the whole thing—then what happens? When we remove the division between the "me" and the "you," the "we" and the "they," what happens? Only then and not before, can one perhaps use the word "love." And love is that most extraordinary thing that takes place when there is no "me" with its circle or wall.

Questioner: When I try to observe myself, why do I find myself observing from the outside, as it were?

KRISHNAMURTI: Have you ever observed a cloud? If you have watched it, you will see that there is not only the physical separation from it, with distance and time, but also that inwardly there is a division. That is to say, your mind is so occupied with other things that you do not give real attention to it; you know all the words one uses, "how beautiful," "how lovely," but all these verbal statements act as a barrier which prevents you from really looking at the cloud. Right? Now can one look at that cloud nonverbally, that is, without the image that one has about clouds? Since it is an objective thing over there, perhaps one may do it fairly easily, but can one look at oneself nonverbally? This means to remove the barriers of criticism, judgment and condemnation and just observe. With a mind free of condemnation and judgment and all the rest of it, then surely the space between you and the thing observed disappears: then you are not there, looking over the wall. You are that. And when you are that, there comes a difficulty. Before, you observed it as something separate from yourself, whereas now you observe it without that separation. But any movement you make with regard to that must still be a movement from the outside. But if you look at it *without any movement*—that is, look at it in complete silence—then that which is observed out of silence is not the same as it was when you looked at it over the wall.

Questioner: (inaudible).

KRISHNAMURTI: A man who is poor and has to work ten hours a day is obviously conditioned, and although he may change slightly, there is no inward revolution because he is stamped by the society in which he lives. Now what is that man to do? Is that your question, Sir?

Questioner: What am I to do in relation to that man?

KRISHNAMURTI: You ask what your relationship is to that man. May I put it differently? What is the relationship between you and me? I have talked, as I have done most of my life, and the day after tomorrow I go away. Now what is our relationship? Have we any relationship? You will obviously have an image of the speaker: what he said or didn't say, whether you agreed or disagreed, and so on. Is there any relationship at all? And is there actually any relationship between a man who is alive, alert, active, inwardly aflame, and the man who says, "Please leave me alone, for God's sake, I am caught in the trap of society and cannot change." One's relationship to such a man can be either affectionate or compassionate—not patronizing. If one is alive and aware of all these things that are happening inside and outside, one does change oneself. And it is always the intelligent minority which, in turn, changes the structure of society and the world. Then, perhaps, there may be a chance for another.

Questioner: This inward psychological revolution that you have talked about: it hasn't taken place in me or in any of my friends, nor, as far as I can see, in many people in history. When I try to look at "what is" and when I see "what is," it still doesn't happen. Yet you seem to hold out hope that it can happen and this hope of yours seems to me, therefore, to be in contradiction to "what is."

KRISHNAMURTI: I hope I am not offering anybody any hope. (*Laughter*) That would be a most terrible thing. If you are looking for hope—from me or from another—then you are avoiding the despair which is what actually is. Do please follow this. Can you look at that despair, which is what actually is—not the hope which is merely a supposition, something you wish for—but actually look at the fear and despair? Can you look at it without hope and without condemnation? Can you see it actually as it is, be directly in contact with it? This means looking at it non-verbally, without any fear, without any distortion. Can you do it? If you can look at "what is" absolutely without any distortion, you will see that the whole thing undergoes a tremendous change: it is no longer despair, it is something entirely different. But, unfortunately, most of us are conditioned and we are always hoping for the ideal, which is an escape. Putting away all escapes, all hopes—not in bitterness or with cynicism but because you see that there is only this fear and despair—then you are left free to look. And when the mind is free, is there despair?

Questioner: Is sex always an escape?

KRISHNAMURTI: I wouldn't know. (*Laughter*) Is it to you? You see, that's just it: it becomes an escape when it is the only thing wherein you feel free of your daily misery, effort and contradiction; and so it becomes a door through which you can escape. And if you do so escape, that very escape breeds fear. But if you are aware that it is an escape, then everything changes.

4

This is our last talk. Do you still wish the subject of medi-tation to be talked about, as was previously suggested?

Audience: Yes.

KRISHNAMURTI: Before we go into it, I think we should consider the question of passion and beauty. The word "passion" is derived from a word meaning "to suffer," but we are using that word in a sense different from either sor-row or lust. Without passion one cannot do very much, and passion is necessary to go into this very complex ques-tion of what meditation is. In the sense we mean—and perhaps we may be giving it a different significance—passion comes when there is the total abandonment of the "me" and the "you," the "we" and the "they," and when, with that abandonment, there is a deep sense of austerity. We do not mean the austerity of the priest or the monk, whose austerity is harsh, directed and sustained through control and suppression. We are talking about a passion that is the outcome of an austerity which is not harsh. An austere mind is really a beautiful mind. Beauty, again, is rather a complex question. In our lives there is so little of it: we live here in a beautiful building surrounded by a lovely wood with marvelous old trees, with the skies blue and with lovely sunsets, but beauty is not the essence of experience. Beauty is not in the thing that man alone has created. To perceive what is deeply beautiful, there must not only be a silence of the mind but also great space in the mind. I hope all this does not sound rather absurd, but I think it will become intelligible as we go along.

We have so very little space in ourselves. Our minds are limited, narrow, shallow, concerned about ourselves and committed to various forms of activities—social, personal, idealistic and so on. While there is a certain space between the observer and the thing observed and also around and within this wall of resistance which constitutes the "me," there is another space that is not bound by either the center or by the wall of resistance. And that space, together with beauty and passion, is essential for an understanding of what meditation is. And, if you will, we will go into that.

Now the West has its own word, "contemplation," but I do not see this as being the same as meditation as it is understood in the East. First of all, then, let us discard what is generally understood by the word meditation, that is, that through meditation one receives a great result, a great experience. Later we may examine the truth or falseness of that idea. The meaning of the word meditation is to ponder, think over, consider, examine in a deeper sense, to feel one's way into something not completely understood, to feel one's way into the mystery and the secret recesses of one's own unexplored mind and depths of feeling. Meditation then, in the real meaning of that word, has its own peculiar beauty, and we are also talking about

124

it as quite one of the most extraordinary things in life—if one knows all that it means. Such meditation transcends all experience. It is not a mystical, romantic or sentimental affair; it needs, rather, a tremendous foundation of right-eousness, of virtue and order. Also, one has to understand the whole question of experience. And so one has to go not only verbally into it, but also feel one's way into something that cannot be conveyed by mere words. It is not some visionary, mystical state induced by thought, but something that comes about naturally and easily when the foundation of righteous behavior is laid. Without that foundation, meditation becomes merely an escape, a fantasy, a thing that one enjoys as a means to some fantastic measures and experiences.

So we are going to go into this question of meditation. And one should, because it is as important as love, death and living—perhaps much more—because out of that meditative mind there comes an understanding of what truth is. Initially we should, I feel, be quite clear as to the falseness or truth of what is generally accepted about medi-tation both in the East and, lately, here in this country. In the East, it is generally understood as a practice in which there is control of thought, such control being based on a particular method or system. There are numbers of these systems in India and also in the Buddhist world, including Zen. Systems and methods are offered in the practicing of which one comes to that state of silence in which reality is revealed. That, in general, is what is understood by the various forms of meditation.

Are you interested in all this? I cannot think why be-cause I am really not interested in it all. (*Laughter*)

There are systems invented by the swamis, yogis, ma-harishis and all the rest of them; meditations upon a series of words and their meanings, or on a phrase, a picture, an image or some quotation which is supposed to have great meaning. And there is also what is called "mantra yoga," which has been introduced into this country and in which you repeat certain Sanskrit words which the guru gives to the disciple in secrecy. These you repeat three or four times a day, or a hundred or a thousand times, whatever it is, thus quieting the mind and enabling you to transcend this

125

world into a different world. Obviously the repetition of a series of words—whether in Sanskrit, Latin, English, or even, if you will, Greek or Chinese—would produce a certain quietness in the mind, a certain quality in the repetitive word tending to make a mind, which is already dull, even duller. (*Laughter*) No, Sirs, please don't laugh; it is quite serious because this is one of the things, with variations, that is practiced a great deal in the East, the idea being that a mind that wanders endlessly is made quiet by repetition. So then the word becomes very important, especially when it is in Sanskrit, because that is an extraordinary language, possessing a certain tonality and quality; and it is hoped that thereby you achieve something. Now you can repeat a word like "Coca Cola" or "Pepsi Cola"—whatever you will—and you will also have an extraordinary feeling. (*Laughter*) So you can see that such repetition as is being done not only in the East, but also in the Catholic churches and monasteries, makes the mind rather shallow, empty and dull. It does not bring to it a sensitivity, a quality of perception. Again, the man who repeats, sees what he wants to see. So we can discard that particular form of what is called meditation—and discard it intelligently, not because someone says so, but because one can see that, by repetition, the mind obviously must become rather dull and insensitive. Please know that the speaker is in no way persuading you to any particular method or system—he doesn't believe in it; there is no method for meditation, as you will see presently.

Then again, other systems lay down a whole series of postures, as a result of which, if you sit rightly, cross-legged and breathing deeply, you will silence the mind. There is a story of a great teacher who is puttering about in the garden when a disciple approaches and sits down, assuming the ordained posture, and looks to the master to instruct him further. So the master sits beside him and, as he sits, he watches the disciple who, by now, has closed his eyes and begun to breathe deeply. Whereupon the teacher asks, "What are you doing, my friend?" The disciple replies, "I am trying to reach the highest consciousness." Then the teacher picks up two pebbles and begins to rub them together. And as he rubs, the disciple, who is on the highest

126

plane of consciousness, opens his eyes and, upon observing what the master is doing, asks, "Master, what are you doing?" The master replies, "I am rubbing two stones together to make one of them into a mirror." So the disciple laughs and says, "Master, you can do that for the next ten thousand years and you will never make a mirror out of a stone." Whereupon the master retorts, "You can sit like that for the next ten thousand years and you will never achieve what you want!"

So there are these systems of breathing and right posture. It is obvious that, in sitting straight or lying down flat, the blood flows more easily to the head, whereas too much bending tends to restrict the flow—that is the idea of sitting straight. Breathing regularly does bring about more oxygen in the blood and therefore quietens the body, and we can gauge the importance or unimportance of it. The idea is that if you practice the method laid down by the guru, you will daily achieve a greater degree of understanding, or of silence, getting closer to heaven, closer to the greatest thing on earth or beyond the earth. The guru is supposed to be enlightened and knows more than the disciple. The word "guru" in Sanskrit means the one who points; like a signpost, he just points. He doesn't tell you what to do. He doesn't even take you by the hand and lead you: he just points the way, leaving you to do with it what you will. But that word has become corrupted by those who use it for themselves, because such gurus offer methods.

Now, what is a method, a system? Please follow this closely because by discarding what is false—that is, through negation—one finds out what is true. That is what we are doing. Without negating totally that which is obviously false, one cannot arrive at any form of understanding. Those of you who have practiced certain systems or forms of meditation can question it for yourselves. When you practice something regularly day after day, getting up at two and three in the morning as the monks do in the Catholic world, or sitting down quietly at certain times during the day, controlling yourself and shaping your thought according to the system or the method, you can ask yourself what you are achieving. You are, in fact, pursuing a method that promises a reward. And when you practice a method day after day, your mind obviously becomes mechanical. There is no freedom in it. A method implies that it is a way laid down by somebody who is supposed to know what he is doing. And—if I may say so—if you are not sufficiently intelligent to see through that, then you will be caught in a mechanical process. That is, the daily practicing, the daily polishing, making your life into a routine so that gradually, ultimately—it may take five, ten or any number of years—you will be in a state to understand what truth is, what enlightenment and reality are and so on. Quite obviously no method can do that because method implies a practice; and a mind that practices something day after day becomes mechanical, loses its quality of sensitivity and its freshness. So again one can see the falseness of the systems offered. Then there are other systems, including Zen and the various occult systems wherein the methods are revealed only to the few. The speaker has met with some of those but discarded them right from the beginning as having no meaning.

So, through close examination, understanding and intelligence, one can discard the mere repetition of words and one can discard altogether the guru—he who stands for authority, the one who knows as against the one who does not know. The guru or the man who says he knows, does *not* know. You cannot ever know what truth is because it is a living thing, whereas a method, a path, lays down the steps to be taken in order to reach truth—as though truth is something that is fixed and permanent, tied down for your convenience. So if you will discard authority completely—not partially but *completely*, including that of the speaker—then you will also discard, quite naturally, all systems and the mere repetition of words.

Having discarded all that, perhaps we can now proceed to find out what the meditative mind is. As we pointed out, there must be a foundation of righteous behavior, not as the pursuit of an idea which is considered righteous, the practicing of which in daily life becomes mere respectability and therefore far from righteous. That which is respectable, accepted by society as moral, is not moral: it is unrighteous. Do you accept all this?

Do you know, Sirs, what it means to be moral, to be

virtuous? You may dislike those two words, but to be really moral is to end all respectability—the respectability which society recognizes as being moral. You can be ambitious, greedy, envious, jealous, full of violence, competitive, destructive, exhorted to kill, and society will consider all that moral and therefore very respectable. We, however, are talking of a different morality and virtue altogether, something which has nothing to do with social morality. Virtue is order, but not order according to a design or blueprint, something laid down by the church, by society or by your own ideological principles. Virtue means order. Order means the understanding of what disorder is and freeing the mind from that disorder—the disorder of resistance, of greed, envy, brutality and fear. And out of that comes a virtue which is not something cultivated by thought, as humility is something that cannot be cultivated by thought. A mind which is vain can endeavor to cultivate humility, hoping thereby to mask its own vanity, but such a mind has no humility. Similarly virtue is a living thing that is not the result of a practice, that is not dependent on environmental influence; it is a behavior which is righteous, true and deeply honest. Most of us are dishonest. Those who have ideals and pursue them are essentially dishonest because they are not what they are pretending to be. So, one has to lay this foundation, and the manner in which it is laid is of greater importance than understanding what meditation is: indeed, this very manner of laying *is* meditation. If in that laying, there is any resistance, suppression or control, then it ceases to be righteous because in all that effort is involved; and effort, as we said yesterday, comes about only when there is contradiction in oneself.

So, is it possible for the mind to recognize that the morality practiced in the world is not really moral at all; and, in the understanding of that, the seeing of its envy, greed and acquisitiveness, to be free of it without effort? Do I make myself clear? That is, seeing the totality of envy, not just a particular form of it but the whole meaning of it, seeing it not only as an idea but in actuality, then that very act of seeing frees the mind from envy. And therefore, in that freedom, there is no conflict. Righteousness, then, cannot be the outcome of conflict and is not the result of a drilled mind. In a mind which understands what it is to learn (which is the understanding of "what is"), the learning itself brings about its own discipline; and such discipline is extraordinarily austere. So there it is: if you have laid the foundation in that manner, then we can proceed, but if you are not virtuous in that deep sense of the word, then meditation becomes an escape, a dishonest activity. Even a stupid mind, a dull mind, can make itself quiet through drugs or the repetition of words, but to be righteous demands a great sensitivity and therefore a great austerity—not of the ashes and loincloth variety, which again is a pretension and an outward show—but to be inwardly and deeply austere. Such austerity has great beauty: it is like fine steel.

In the understanding of ourselves, obviously, lie the beginnings of meditation. This understanding of oneself is quite a complex affair. There is the conscious mind and the unconscious—the so-called deep or hidden mind. I don't know why such great importance has been given to the unconscious. It is the treasure of the past—if that can be called a treasure. The racial inheritance, the tradition, the memories, the motives, the concealed demands, urges, desires, pursuits and compulsions. The conscious mind obviously cannot, through analysis, explore all the unconscious, those deep, hidden, secret layers of the mind, because it would take many years. Moreover, a conscious mind that undertakes to examine the unconscious must itself be extraordinarily alert, unconditioned, sharp and of unbiased perception. So it becomes quite a problem. It is said that the unconscious reveals itself through dreams and intimations, and that you must dream, otherwise you would go mad. Does one ever ask why one should dream at all? We have accepted that we must dream. As you know, we are the most tradition-bound people; despite being very modern and greatly sophisticated, we accept tradition and are "yes sayers." We never say "no," never doubt, never question. Some authority or specialist comes along and says this or that and we promptly agree, saying, "Right, Sir, you know better than we do." But we are going to question this whole matter of the unconscious, the conscious and dreams.

Why should you dream at all? Obviously because during the day your conscious mind is so occupied with the job, with the quarrels, with the family, the various items of possible amusement. All the time it is chattering away endlessly, talking to itself, counting—you know all that it does. And so at night, when the brain is somewhat quieter, and the whole body more peaceful, the deeper layers are supposed to project their contents into the mind, giving hints and intimations of what it hopes you will understand, and so on. Have you ever tried, during the day, to be watchful without correction, aware without choice, watching your thought, your motives, what you are saying, how you are sitting, the manner of your usage of words, your gestures—watching? Have you ever tried? If, during the day, you have watched without attempting to correct, not saying to yourself, "What a terrible thought that is, I mustn't have it," but just watching, then you will see that having uncovered, during the day, your motives, demands and urges, when you come to sleep at night, your mind and your brain are quieter. And you will also find, as you go into it very deeply, that no dreams are possible. As a result, when it wakes up, the mind finds itself extraordinarily alive, active, fresh and innocent. I wonder if you will attempt to do all these things or whether all this is just a lot of words.

Then there is the other problem. The mind, as we have it, is always calculating, comparing, pursuing, driven, endlessly chattering to itself or gossiping about somebody else —you know what it does every day and all day long. Such a mind cannot possibly see what is true or perceive what is false. Such perception is only possible when the mind is quiet. When you want to listen to what the speaker is saying—if you are interested—your mind is naturally quiet: it ceases to chatter or think about something else. If you want to see something very clearly—if you want to understand your wife or your husband, or to see the cloud in all its glory and beauty—you look, and the looking must be out of silence, otherwise you cannot see. So, can the mind, which is so endlessly moving, chattering, chasing and taking fright, ever be quiet? Not through drill, suppression or control, but just be quiet?

The professional meditators tell us to control. Now control implies not only the one who controls but also the thing controlled. As you watch your mind, your thought wanders off and you pull it back; then it wanders again and

131

again you pull it back. So this game goes on endlessly. And if, at the end of ten years or whatever it is, you can control so completely that your mind does not wander at all and has no thoughts whatever, then, it is said, you will have achieved a most extraordinary state. But actually, on the contrary, you will not have achieved anything at all. Control implies resistance. Please follow this a little. Concentration is a form of resistance, the narrowing down of thought to a particular point. And when the mind is being trained to concentrate completely on one thing, it loses its elasticity, its sensitivity, and becomes incapable of grasping the total field of life.

Now is it possible for a mind to have this sense of concentration without exclusion, and yet without resorting to subjugation, conformity or suppression for purposes of control? It is very easy to concentrate; every schoolboy learns it—though he hates doing it, he is forced to try to concentrate. And when you do concentrate, you are surely resisting; your whole mind is focused on something and if you train it day after day to concentrate on one thing, naturally it loses its sharpness, its width, its depth, and it has no space. So the problem then is: can the mind possess this quality of concentration—although that really isn't the word—this quality of paying attention to one thing without losing the total attention? By "total attention" we mean that attention which is given with your whole mind, in which there is no fear, no pain, no profit motive, no pleasure—because you have already understood what the implications of pleasure are. So when the mind thus gives attention completely—that is, with your heart, your nerves, your eyes, your whole being—then such attention can also include attention given to one small item. When you wash dishes, you can give complete attention to it without this resistance, this narrowing down associated with ordinary concentration.

So, having seen the necessity for laying the foundation naturally, without any distortion, without any effort and discarding all authority, we can now consider the search by the mind for experience. Most of us lead such a dull, routine life of obviously very little meaning, that, through various forms of stimuli including drugs, we constantly seek wider and deeper experiences. Now, when one has an experience, the recognition of it as an experience shows that you must already have had it, otherwise you would not recognize it. So the Christian, conditioned as he is to the worship of a particular Savior, when taking drugs or seeking some great experience through different ways, will obviously see something colored by his own conditioning, and therefore what he sees will be his own projection. And although that may be most extraordinary, with great luminosity, depth and beauty, it will still be his own background being projected. Therefore the mind that seeks experience as a means of giving significance and meaning to life, is, in reality, projecting its own background, whereas the mind that is not seeking because it is free, has quite a different quality.

Now all that has been observed, from the beginning of this talk until now, is part of meditation; to see the truth as we go along; to see the falseness of the guru, the authority, the system; to lay the foundation of a behavior which is not the mere outcome of environment and in which there is no effort at all. All that implies a quality of meditation. When one is at that point, having understood this whole business of living in which there is no conflict at all, one can then proceed to inquire into what silence is. If you inquire without having done all the previous things, your silence will have no meaning whatsoever, for without a true understanding of beauty, of love, of death and of virtue, a mind must remain shallow, and any silence that it produces will be silence of death. But if you have taken the journey with the speaker this evening, as I hope you have, then we can proceed to ask, "What is silence, what is the quality of silence?" Remember that if one wants to see anything very clearly, without any effort and without any distortion, the mind must be quiet. If I want to see your face, if I want to listen to the beauty of your voice, if I want to see what kind of person you are, my mind must be quiet and not chatter. If it is chattering and wandering all over the place, then I am unable to see either your beauty or your ugliness. So silence is necessary for such seeing, as night is necessary for the day; also that silence is neither the product of noise nor of the cessation of noise. That silence comes naturally when all the other qualities have come into being.

You know, Sirs, in that silence there is space, but not the space that exists between the observer and the thing observed—as, for instance, between me and this microphone (without which I could not see it). A silent mind has great space not created by either the object or the observer. I do not know if you have ever watched what space is: there is space displaced by and around this microphone; there is space around the "me" and around the "you." Whenever we say "we" and "they," there is this space which we have created around ourselves. When you say you are Christian, Catholic, Protestant or Communist, there is space according to how you thus limit yourself, and that space inevitably breeds conflict because it is limited and because it divides. But when there is silence, there is not the space of division, but quite a different quality of space. And there must be such space, as only then can come that which is not measurable by thought—that immensity, that which is supreme and which cannot be invited. A petty mind, practicing indefinitely, still remains petty. Most people who are seeking truth are actually inviting truth, but truth cannot be invited. The mind has not enough space and is not sufficiently quiet. So meditation is from the beginning to the end, and in meditation lies the skill in action.

So, all this is meditation. If you can do this, the door is open, and it is for you to come to it. What lies beyond is not something romantic or emotional, something that you wish for, something to which you can escape. But you come to it with a full mind which is intelligent, sensitive and without any distortion. You come to it with great love, otherwise meditation has no meaning.

Questioner: In the middle of your talk you mentioned that although meditation wasn't what you wanted to talk about, it was necessary to talk about it. Was there some other subject?

KRISHNAMURTI: Sir, what didn't interest me was the explanation of the obvious, the obvious being the methods, the systems, the repetition of words, the gurus—all so obvious. What *is* important is not to follow anybody but to under-

134

stand oneself. If you go into yourself without effort, fear, without any sense of restraint, and really delve deeply, you will find extraordinary things; and you don't have to read a single book. The speaker has not read a single book about any of these things: philosophy, psychology, sacred books. In oneself lies the whole world, and if you know how to look and learn, then the door is there and the key is in your hand. Nobody on earth can give you either that key or the door to open, except yourself.

Questioner: Is there a reason for being?

KRISHNAMURTI: Why do you want a reason for being? (*Laughter*) You are here. And because you are here and don't understand yourself, you want to invent a reason. You know, Sir, when you look at a tree or the clouds, the light on the water, when you know what it means to love, you will require no reason for being: you are, there is. Then all the museums in the world and all the concerts will have only secondary importance. Beauty is there for you to see, if you have the mind and the heart to look—not out there in the cloud, in the tree, in the water, in the thing, but in yourself.

TALK AT THE UNIVERSITY OF CALIFORNIA AT SANTA CRUZ

This evening I would like to talk about several things which are all related, just as all human problems are also related. One cannot take one problem separately and try to solve it by itself; each problem contains all the other problems, if one knows how to go into it deeply and comprehensively.

I would, first of all, like to ask what is going to become of all of us, the young and the old, what will we make of our lives? Are we going to allow ourselves to be sucked into this maelstrom of accepted respectability with its social and economic morality, and become part of the so-called cultural society with all its problems, its confusion and contradiction, or are we going to make something entirely different of our life? That is the problem which faces most people. One is educated, not to understand life as a whole, but to play a particular role in this totality of existence. We are so heavily conditioned from childhood to achieve something in this society, to be successful and to become a complete bourgeois; and the more sensitive intellectual generally revolts against such a pattern of existence. In his revolt, he does various things: either he becomes antisocial, antipolitical, takes to drugs and pursues some narrow, sectarian, religious belief, following some guru, some teacher or philosopher, or he becomes an activist, a Communist, or he gives himself over entirely to some exotic religion like Buddhism or Hinduism. And by becoming a sociologist, a scientist, an artist, a writer or, if one has the capacity, a philosopher and, thereby, enclosing oneself in a circle, we think we have solved the problem. We then imagine we have understood the whole of life and we dictate to others what life should be according to our own particular tendency, our own particular idiosyncrasy, and from our own specialized knowledge.

When one observes what life is with its enormous complexity and intricacy, not only in the economic and social spheres, but also in the psychological sphere, one must ask oneself, if one is at all serious, what part one is to play in all this. What shall I do as a human being living in this world and not escaping into some fantasy existence or a monastery?

Seeing this whole pattern very clearly, what is one to do, what is one to make of one's life? This question is always there, whether we are well placed in the establishment or just about to enter into it. So, it seems to me, one must inevitably ask this question: What is the purpose of life and as a fairly healthy human being psychologically, who is not totally neurotic and who is alive and active, what part shall I play in all this? Which role or which part am I attracted to? And, if I am attracted to a particular fragment or section, then I must be aware of the danger in such an attraction, because we are back again in the same old division which breeds effort, contradiction and war. Can I then take part in the whole of life and not in just one particular segment of it? To take part in the whole of life obviously does not mean to have a complete knowledge of science, sociology, philosophy, mathematics, and so on; that would be impossible unless one were a genius.

Can one, therefore, bring about psychologically, inwardly, a totally different way of living? This obviously means that one takes an interest in all the outward things, but that the fundamental, radical revolution is in the psychological realm. What can one do to bring about such a change deeply within oneself? For oneself is the society, is the world, is all the content of the past. So the problem is: How can we, you and I, take part in the *totality* of life and not merely in one segment of it? That's one problem; there are also the problems of conduct, behavior and virtue and the problem of love—what love is, and what death is. Whether we are young or old, we must ask ourselves these questions, because they are part of life, part of our existence; and together, if you are agreeable, we must talk over these problems this evening. We are going into these problems together; you are not outside of all this, merely a spectator, a listener observing with curiosity and taking a casual interest. Whether we like it or not, we are all involved in this inquiry—what to make of our life, what is righteous behavior, what is love (if there is such a thing), what is the meaning of that extraordinary thing called death, which most people won't even discuss. So, seeing the whole of this, one must ask what is the purpose of all existence.

The life that we lead at present has actually very little meaning, passing a few examinations, getting a degree, finding a good job and struggling for the rest of our life until we die. And to invent a meaning to this utter disorder is equally disastrous. Now what is possible for us, seeing all this and knowing that there must be a deep, psychological revolution to bring about a different order, a different society, and at the same time not depending on *anyone* to give us enlightenment or clarity—so what is possible? To find out what is possible, one must, first of all, find out what is impossible. Now what is impossible or appears to be impossible? It appears impossible for a complete change, a complete psychological revolution to take place *immediately*, that is, tomorrow you wake up and you are completely different, your way of looking, thinking, feeling is so new, so alive, so passionate, so true, that in it there is no longer a shadow of conflict or hypocrisy. You say that is impossible because you have accepted or become accustomed to the idea of psychological evolution, a gradual change which may take fifty years; so time is necessary, not only chronological time but psychological time. That is the accepted, traditional way of thinking; to change, to bring about a radical, psychological revolution, time is necessary. If one suggests, as the speaker does, that it *is* possible to change completely by tomorrow, you would say that is impossible, wouldn't you? So, for you, that is the impossible; now from knowing what is impossible, you can find out what is possible. The possibility then is not the same as it was before: it's entirely different. Are we following each other?

When we say this is possible, that is impossible, the possibility is measurable, but when we realize something which is impossible, then we see in relation to the impossible what is possible; and that possibility then is entirely different from what was possible before. Please, listen carefully, don't compare this with what somebody else has said, just watch it in yourself and you will see an extraordinary thing takes place. The possibility now, as we are, is very small; it is possible to go to the moon, to become a rich man or a professor, whatever it is, but that possibility is very trivial. Now when you are confronted with an issue such as this, that you must change completely by tomorrow and therefore become a totally different human being, then you are faced with the impossible. When you realize the impossibility of that, then in relation to the impossible, you will find out what is possible, which is something entirely different; therefore quite a different possibility takes place in your mind. And it is this possibility that we are talking about, not the trivial possibility. So, bearing all this in mind, the impossible and the possible in relationship to the impossible, and seeing this whole pattern of existence, what can I do? The impossible is to love without a shadow of jealousy and hate.

Most of us, I am afraid, are terribly jealous, envious and possessive. When you love somebody, your girlfriend, your wife or your husband, you are determined to hold them for the rest of your life; at least you try to. And you call that "love"—he or she is "mine." And when "the mine" looks away or looks at another, becomes somewhat independent, then there is fury, jealousy and anxiety, then all the misery of what is called love begins.

Now, what is it to love without a shadow of all that?

No doubt, you would consider it impossible, you would consider it inhuman, in fact superhuman—so, to you it is impossible. If you see the impossibility of that, then you will find out what is possible in relationship. I hope I am making myself clear. That is the first point.

Secondly, our life, as it is now, is struggle, pain, pleasure, fear, anxiety, uncertainty, despair, war, hatred—you know what our everyday living actually is, the competition, the destruction, the disorder. This is actually what is taking place, not what "should be" or what "ought to be"; we are only concerned with *what is*. So, seeing all this, we say to ourselves: "It's too awful, I must escape from it! I want a wider, deeper, more extensive vision. I want to become more sensitive." Therefore we take drugs.

This question of drugs is very old; they have been taking drugs in India for thousands of years. At one time it was called soma, now it is hashish and pan; they haven't yet reached the highly sophisticated level of LSD, but they probably will very soon now. People take hashish and pan in order to become less sensitive; they get lost in the perfume of it, in the different visions it produces and accentuates. These drugs are generally taken by the laborers, the manual workers (here you do not have "untouchables" as they are called in India). They take drugs because their lives are dreadfully dull; they have not much food, so they haven't much energy. The only two things they have are sex and drugs.

The truly religious man, the man who really wants to find out what truth is, what life is—not from books, not from religious entertainers, not from philosophers who only stimulate intellectually—such a man will have nothing whatever to do with drugs, because he knows full well that they distort the mind, making it incapable of finding out what truth is.

Here in the Western world many people are resorting to drugs. There are the serious ones who have taken it experimentally for perhaps a couple of years, some of whom have come to see me. They have said: "We have had experiences which appear—from what we have read in books—to resemble the ultimate reality, to be a shadow of the real." And because they are serious people, as the speaker is, they have discussed this problem deeply; ultimately they have been forced to admit that the experience is very spurious, that it has nothing whatever to do with the ultimate reality, with all the beauty of that immensity. Unless a mind is clear, wholesome and completely healthy, it cannot possibly be in the state of religious meditation which is absolutely essential to discover that thing which is beyond all thought, beyond all desire. Any form of psychological dependence, any kind of escape, through drink, through drugs, in an attempt to make the mind more sensitive merely dulls and distorts it.

When you discard all that—as one must if one is at all serious—you are faced with living inwardly alone. Then you are not depending on anything or anybody, on any drug, on any book, or on any belief. Only then is the mind unafraid, only then can you ask what is the purpose of life. And if you have come to that point, would you ask such a question? The purpose of life is *to live*—not in the utter chaos and confusion that we call living—but to live in an entirely different way, to live a life that is full, to live a life that is complete, to live that way today. That is the true meaning of life—to live, not heroically, but to live so completely inwardly, without fear, without struggle and without all the rest of the misery.

It is possible only when you know what is impossible; you must, therefore, see whether you can change immediately, say, with regard to anger, hate and jealousy, so that you are no longer jealous, which is, of course, envious; envy being a comparison between yourself and another. Now, is it possible to change so completely that envy doesn't touch you at all? This is only possible when you are aware of the envy without this division of the observer and the observed, so that you *are* envy, you *are* that: not you and envy as something separate from you. Therefore, when you see this whole thing completely, there is no possibility of doing any-

142

thing about it; and when there is this complete state of envy, in which there is no division and no conflict, then it is no longer envy; it is something entirely different.

One can then ask: What is love? Is love pleasure? Is love desire? Is love the product of thought, as pleasure is and fear is? Can love be cultivated and will love come about through time? And, if I don't know what love is, can I come upon it?

Love is obviously not sentimentality or emotionalism, so they can be brushed aside immediately, because sentimentality and emotionalism are romantic, and love is not romanticism. Now pleasure and fear are the movement of thought and for most of us pleasure is the greatest thing in life; sexual pleasure and the memory of it, the thought of having had that pleasure, thinking about it over and over again and wanting it tomorrow—the morality of society is based on pleasure. So, if pleasure is not love, then what is love? Please follow this, because *you* have to answer these questions; you can't just wait for the speaker or somebody else to tell you. This is a fundamental, human question that must be answered by each one of us, not by some guru or philosopher who says this is love, that is not love.

Love is not jealousy or envy, is it? You are all very silent! Can you love and at the same time be greedy, ambitious, competitive? Can you love when you kill not only animals but also other human beings? Through the negation of what love is *not*—it is not jealousy, envy, hate, the self-centered activity of the "me" and the "you," the ugly competition, the brutality and the violence of everyday life—you will know what love is. When you put all these things aside, not intellectually but actually, with your heart, with your mind, with your—I was going to say guts, because obviously all this is not love, then you will come upon love. When you know love, when you have love, then you are free to do what is right; and whatever you do is righteous.

But to come to that state, to have that sense of beauty and compassion which love brings, there must also be the death of yesterday. The death of yesterday means to die to everything inwardly, to all ambition and everything that psychologically one has accumulated. After all, when death comes, that's what is going to happen anyway; you are going to leave your family, your house, your goods, your valuables, all the things you possess. You are going to leave all the books from which you have derived so much knowledge, as well as the books you wanted to write and have not written, and the pictures you wanted to paint. When you die to all that, then the mind is completely new, fresh and innocent. I suppose you will say it is impossible.

When you say it is impossible, then you begin to invent theories; there must be a life after death; according to the Christians there is resurrection, while the whole of Asia believes in reincarnation. The Hindus maintain that it is impossible to die to everything while one still has life and health and beauty; so fearing death, they give hope by inventing this wonderful thing called reincarnation, which means that the next life will be better. However, the better has a string attached to it; to be better in my next life, I must be good in this one, therefore I must behave myself. I must live righteously; I must not hurt another; there must be no anxiety, no violence. But unfortunately these believers in reincarnation do not live that way; on the contrary, they are aggressive, as full of violence as everyone else, so their belief is as worthless as the dead yesterdays.

The important thing is what you are now, and not whether you believe or don't believe, whether your experiences are psychedelic or merely ordinary. What matters is to live at the height of virtue (I know you don't like that word). Those two words "virtue" and "righteousness" have been terribly abused, every priest uses them, every moralist or idealist employs them. But virtue is entirely different from something which is practiced as virtue and therein lies its beauty; if you try to practice it, then it is no longer virtue. Virtue is not of time, so it cannot be practiced and behavior is not dependent on environment; environmental behavior is all right in its way but it has no virtue. Virtue means to love, to have no fear, to live at the highest level of existence, which is to die to everything, inwardly, to die to the past, so that the mind is clear and innocent. And it is only such a mind that can come upon this extraordinary immensity which is not your own invention, nor that of some philosopher or guru.

Questioner: Will you please explain the difference between thought and insight?

KRISHNAMURTI: Do you mean by "insight" understanding? To see something very clearly, to have no confusion, no choice? I want to understand in what way you are using that word "insight." Is that correct, Sir?

Questioner: Yes.

KRISHNAMURTI: What is thinking? Please, let's go into this! When I ask you that question "What is thinking," what takes place in your mind?

Questioner: Thought.

KRISHNAMURTI: Go slowly, Sir, step by step, don't rush at it! What takes place? I ask you a question. I ask you where you live or what's your name. Your answer is immediate, isn't it? Why?

Questioner: Because you are dealing with something in the past.

KRISHNAMURTI: Please, don't complicate the thing, just look at it! We'll complicate it presently but, first of all, just look at it. (*Laughter*) I ask you your name, your address, where you live and so on. The answer is immediate because you are familiar with it, you don't have to think about it. Probably you thought about it at first, but you've been brought up since childhood to know your name. There is no thought process involved in that. Now, next time I ask you something a little more difficult and there is a time lag between the question and your answer. What takes place in that interval? Go slowly, don't answer *me* but find out for yourself. All right, I'll ask you a question: What is the distance from here to the moon, to Mars or to New York? In that interval what takes place?

Questioner: Searching.

KRISHNAMURTI: You're searching, aren't you? Searching where?

Questioner: My memory.

KRISHNAMURTI: You're searching your memory, that is, somebody has told you or you have read about it, so you are looking in your "cupboard." (*Laughter*) And then you come up with the answer. To the first question there was an immediate answer, but you are uncertain about the second question, so you take more time. In that interval you are thinking, probing, investigating and eventually you find the right answer. Now, if you are asked a very complex question like "What is God?"

Questioner 1: God is love.

Questioner 2: God is everything.

Questioner 3: The answer isn't in my memory.

KRISHNAMURTI: Just listen! "God is love, God is everything."

Questioner: God is the big furniture remover. (Laughter)

KRISHNAMURTI: And so on. Now watch it, just look what's happened. You never said we don't know which is the right answer. Please, follow this! It is very important. Not knowing, you believe! Look what has happened, thought has betrayed you. First, a familiar question, then a more difficult one, and finally a question to which the mind says I've been conditioned to believe in God, so I have an answer. And if you were a Communist you would say, "What are you talking about? Don't be silly, there's no such thing as God. It's a bourgeois belief invented by the priests!" (*Laughter*) Now, we are talking about thought. First of all,

146

to find out if there is or there is not God (and we must find out, otherwise we are not total human beings), to find that out, all belief, that is, all conditioning brought about by human thought, which arises out of fear must come to an end. We then see what thinking is: thinking is the response of memory, which is your accumulated knowledge, experience and background, and when you are asked a question, certain vibrations are set up, and from that memory you respond. That is thought. Please, watch it in yourself! And thought is always old, obviously, because it responds from the past, therefore thought can never be free. (*Pause*) You don't go along with that, do you? (*Laughter*) "Freedom of thought." Please, look at it very carefully, don't laugh it off! We worship thought, don't we? Thought is the greatest thing in life, the intellectuals adore it, but when you look very closely at the whole process of thought —however reasonable, however logical—it is still the response of memory which is always old, so thought itself is old and can never bring about freedom. Please don't accept what the speaker says about anything!

So, thought then brings confusion. The question was: What is the difference between thought and insight which, we agreed, was the same as understanding, seeing things very clearly, without any confusion. When you see something very clearly—we are talking psychologically—then there is no choice; there is only choice when there is confusion. We say there is freedom to choose which really means there is freedom to be confused, because if you are not confused, if you see something instantly and very clearly, then where is the need to choose? And when there is no choice, there is clarity.

Clarity, insight or understanding are only possible when thought is in abeyance, when the mind is still. Then only can you see very clearly, then you can say you have really understood what we are talking about, then you have direct perception, because your mind is no longer confused. Confusion implies choice and choice is the product of thought. Shall I do this or that—the "me" and the "not me," the "you" and the "not you," "we" and "they," and so on, all that is implied by thought. And out of this arises confusion and from that confusion we choose; we choose our political leaders, our gurus, and so many other things, but when there is clarity, then there is direct perception. And to be clear, the mind must be completely quiet, completely still, then there is real understanding and therefore that understanding is action. It isn't the other way around.

Questioner: How do people become neurotic?

KRISHNAMURTI: How do I know they are neurotic? Please, this is a very serious question, so do listen! How do I know they are neurotic? Am I also neurotic because I recognize that they are neurotic?

Questioner: Yes.

KRISHNAMURTI: Don't say "yes" so quickly! Just look at it, listen to it! Neurotic, what does that mean? A little odd, not clear, confused, slightly off balance? And unfortunately most of us are slightly off balance. No? You aren't quite sure! (*Laughter*) Aren't you off balance if you are a Christian, a Hindu, a Buddhist or a Communist? Aren't you neurotic when you enclose yourself with your problems, build a wall around yourself because you think you are much better than somebody else? Aren't you off balance when your life is full of resistance—the "me" and "you," the "we" and "they" and all the other divisions? Aren't you neurotic in the office when you want to go one better than the other fellow? So, how does one become neurotic? Does society make you neurotic? This is the simplest explanation—my father, my mother, my neighbor, the government, the army, everybody makes me neurotic. They are all responsible for my being off balance. And when I go to the analyst for help, poor chap, he's also neurotic like me. (*Laughter*) Please, don't laugh! This is exactly what is happening in the world. Now why do I become neurotic? Everything in the world as it exists now, the society, the family, the parents, the children—they have no love. Do you think there would be wars if they had love? Do you think there would be governments that consider it is perfectly all right for you to be killed? Such a society would never exist if your mother and father really loved you, cared for you, looked after you and taught you how to be kind to people, how to live and how to love. These are the outer pressures and demands that bring about this neurotic society; there are also the inner compulsions and urges within ourselves, our innate violence inherited from the past, which help to make up this neurosis, this imbalance. So this is the fact—most of us are slightly off balance, or more, and it's no use blaming anybody. The fact is that one is not balanced psychologically, mentally, or sexually; in every way we are off balance. Now the important thing is to become aware of it, to know that one is not balanced, not how to become balanced. A neurotic mind cannot become balanced, but if it has not gone to the extremes of neurosis, if it has still retained some balance, it can watch itself. One can then become aware of what one does, of what one says, of what one thinks, how one moves, how one sits, how one eats, watching all the time but not correcting. And if you watch in such a manner, without any choice, then out of that deep watching will come a balanced, sane, human being; then you will no longer be neurotic. A balanced mind is a mind that is wise, not made up of judgments and opinions.

Questioner: Where does thought end and silence begin?

KRISHNAMURTI: Have you ever noticed a gap between two thoughts? Or are you thinking all the time without an interval? Do you understand the question?

Questioner: No.

KRISHNAMURTI: Is there an interval between two thoughts? Is the question clear?

Questioner: Yes.

KRISHNAMURTI: Or is this the first time you have been asked such a question! I want to find out, Sir, what silence is. Is silence the cessation of noise? Is it like the peace which exists between two wars? Or is it the interval between two thoughts? Or has it nothing whatever to do with any of this? If silence is the cessation of thought, the cessation of noise, then it is fairly easy to suppress noise, that is, noise being chatter—you stop chattering. Is that silence?

Or is silence a state of mind that is no longer confused, no longer afraid. So where does silence begin? Does it begin when thought ends? Have you, ever tried to end thought?

Questioner: When the mind radically changes speed, it is a quiet mind.

KRISHNAMURTI: Yes, Sir, but have you ever tried stopping thought?

Questioner: How do you do it?

KRISHNAMURTI: I don't know, but have you ever tried it? First of all, who is the entity who is trying to stop it?

Questioner: The thinker.

KRISHNAMURTI: It's another thought, isn't it? Thought is trying to stop itself, so there is a battle between the thinker and the thought. Please, watch this conflict very carefully! Thought says, "I must stop thinking because then I shall experience a marvelous state," or whatever the motive may be, so you try to suppress thought. Now the entity that is trying to suppress thought is still part of thought, isn't it? One thought is trying to suppress another thought, so there is conflict, a battle is going on. When I see this as a fact—see it totally, understand it completely, have an insight into it, in the sense that gentleman used the word—then the mind is quiet. This comes about naturally and easily when the mind is quiet to watch, to look, to see.

Questioner: When self-centered activity ceases, what motivates action?

KRISHNAMURTI: Find out first what happens when self-centered activity comes to an end, then you won't ask the question, then you will see the beauty of action in itself, then you won't need a motive, because motive is part of self-centered activity; when that self-centered activity is not, action has no motive and is therefore true, righteous and free.